Petar Opalić
Qualitative and Psychometric Research of Refugees and
Traumatised Subjects in Belgrade

I0130146

Reihe »Forschung psychosozial«

Petar Opalić

Qualitative and Psychometric Research of Refugees and Traumatised Subjects in Belgrade

Psychosozial-Verlag

Bibliografische Information der Deutschen Nationalbibliothek
Die Deutsche Nationalbibliothek verzeichnet diese Publikation in der Deutschen
Nationalbibliografie; detaillierte bibliografische Daten sind im Internet über
<http://dnb.d-nb.de> abrufbar.

Originalausgabe
© 2005 Psychosozial-Verlag
E-Mail: info@psychosozial-verlag.de
www.psychosozial-verlag.de
Umschlagabbildung: Goya: »Was ist das für ein Geschrei?«
Umschlaggestaltung: Christof Röhl
nach Entwürfen des Ateliers Warminski, Büdingen
Satz: Claudia Schmitt, Wetzlar
Printed in Germany
ISBN 978-3-89806-358-6

Contents

Preface

Social circumstances in the Western Balkans have always been complex and contradictory, significantly influenced by various cultures and global centres of political power. Therefore, the Western Balkans continuously remain a battlefield of social misunderstandings and even conflicts. The end of the 20th century was, on the global scene, marked by the disintegration of the communist system and disintegration of the Socialist Federal Republic of Yugoslavia. Former Yugoslavia was, politically speaking, a typical totalitarian creation, which, combined with the above-stated, resulted in several wars that took their toll – tens of thousands of innocent victims on all sides of the conflicts, followed by several waves of refugees, the number of which is expressed in hundreds of thousands. All these were followed by a whole range of socio-pathological phenomena – crime, grey economy, drug abuse, alcoholism, divorces, suicides and other social and psychological indicators of social anomie.

This paper aims at determining, in a scientifically valid, objective and reliable way, mental effects the above-mentioned social crisis leaves on refugees after a relatively long time period of time (on average, eight years have elapsed since the main traumatic events), since refugees are, after those who lost their lives to the conflicts, certainly one of the most affected social groups in one of the countries of the seething Western Balkan region.

In order to determine the mental state of refugees, we compared it to the same status of the somatically traumatised (both at war and in peacetime), and, unavoidably, with the mental state of a part of the population of the same or similar social-demographic features who denied any significant trauma in their lives. Therefore, the study, in various combinations, investigated the subjects comprising refugees (placed at refugee camps, which is believed to be definitely the most unfavourable way of taking care of the expulsed and refugees), wounded during the war in Bosnia and Herzegovina, and, finally, the persons from Belgrade and its vicinity who have been injured in traffic accidents, at work, or in their spare time. The third group of subjects comprised the persons without any experience of trauma whatsoever. The group, of course, was used as a control group. However, it has to be noted that, bearing in mind the stressfulness of general conditions of life and social conditions in Serbia during the nineties, the group could be used at the same time as an experimental one, that is, as the group that could be used to investigate the effects of the general high-risk stress (wars in the region, NATO bombing, external sanctions, economic and political transition, all taking place at the same time) in comparison to the population of the prosperous and peaceful countries experiencing no such problems for a long period of time. Therefore, the group could be an interesting one to the researchers analysing the effects of the overall stressful factors on the mental state of people from a trans-cultural and international point of view.

Taking into account the results obtained by similar researches, we endeavoured to shed some more light on the subjective – more difficult to notice and understand – effects refugeeism as a forceful, multilayered and, in our case, long-term trauma causes in relation to the interior world of an individual. In other words, we endeavoured to determine, in a scientifically and methodologically diverse sense, devastating effects on the mental life of the people exposed to expulsion and compulsion of adjusting to new and more difficult living conditions. The comparison of their mental state with the subjective status of the so-called healthy population of the domicile population of Belgrade, as well as with the subjective status of the somatically traumatised, was aimed at determining the nuances in differences of mental responses to various accidents, especially refugeeism.

Having in mind that the subject matter of the research was the individual's internal world of experience, never comprehensible in its full entirety, we believed that the research should be, in a methodological sense, both qualitative and quantitative. Namely, the former methodological approach is based on the statistical objectivity, precision and reliability of data, primarily psychometric research, while the latter is to provide qualitative depth, that is, to shed some more light on the specificity of mental life of the traumatised. While the former is, despite its reliability and objectivity, neutral and »cold«, the latter method is illustrative and vivid. Both of them are, in their own ways, universally understandable.

Using the human figure drawing as a method of research located somewhere between the analysis of dreams on one side, and the application of the set of psychometric and similar research instruments (such as the PTSD-10 Scale, Brief Eysenck's Personality Inventory, Late Effects of Accidental Injury Questionnaire, Family Homogeneity Index) on the other side, should contribute to the insight into the mental state of the subjects obtained through both qualitative and quantitative research.

Although the sample was varied, depending on the focus of our research of certain parts of the study (some of which have already been published in journals or presented at scientific gatherings), we did not change the theoretic framework of interpretation, which, we believed, was a *conditio sine qua non* of the persuasiveness of the research results' interpretation and discursive integrity of the whole text of the study. The theoretic framework is an existentially-analytical one, already used in our previous papers. It is most outstandingly recognisable in the last chapter, case studies or in biographies of our subjects. Besides, we believe that dreams and human figure drawings of very distinctive or typical subjects, presented *in extenso*, contribute to the authenticity and vividness of presenting the results of quantitative or psychometric data processing, and equally support the stated theoretic position of the study.

Lastly, it is my great pleasure to thank, most of all, my subjects – especially the refugees, the wounded and the injured, who patiently replied to a series of questions taken from several instruments. I am also thankful to my colleagues, Assistant Prof. Dr. Aleksandar Lešić, surgeon of the Orthopaedic Hospital of the University Clinical Centre, Belgrade and Lazar Nikolić, who spared no efforts in helping me test certain parts of the sample. I would also like to express my gratitude to Prof. Dr. Ljubomir Žiropadja, psychologist, for his support in statistical data processing, as well as to all health care workers who supported me, more or less noticeably, in my efforts to publish this study.

I would hereby also like to express my gratitude to Ljiljana Smudja for her contribution to the translation of this book into English.

The author is especially grateful to the Alexander von Humboldt Foundation for their support in various phases of this study, particularly in its publication.

Petar Opalić

9

I

Introductory Deliberations

1. Problems of Refugees in Serbia

The social position of refugees in Serbia

In relation to massive disasters (refugeeism certainly being one), the World Health Organisation (WHO 1992) called attention to the fact that the intensity and other features of trauma did not have an upper limit. On the other hand, when discussing the issue of refugeeism, one must know that it is a complex phenomenon which involves disorders in the psychological, economic, political and social sphere, but primarily in the organisation of one's life. Destructive effects of such a disaster (i.e. refugeeism) are such that they imply harmful consequences which cannot be overcome by regular social measures. Therefore, what is considered a disaster also directly depends on the capacity of the society, culture and times in which it appears to overcome it. More-over, the United Nations have called attention to the fact that if a disaster kept on repeating, it would raise the upper limit above which an event was considered a disas-ter. The World Health Organisation also noted that the so-called disasters caused by human factor (war and the like) produce mental disorders in nearly 30% of popula-tion, which is significantly higher than in so-called natural disasters (earthquakes, floods and the like).

Refugeeism does not imply only the loss of homeland and home (house or apart-ment) and massive material impoverishment, but also the loss of employment. It also dramatically decreases general social security. Besides, refugees in Serbia and Monte-negro are entitled only to health care and education under the same conditions as the citizens of Serbia and Montenegro, without any of the political rights they used to have.

Today, every 10th refugee in the world is from the territory of former Yugoslavia. It is considered that around 3.5 million people had to leave their homes in former Yugoslavia. According to the UNHCR and the International Organisation of the Red Cross, Germany received 320,000 refugees from the territory of former Yugoslavia, Sweden received 86,000, Austria 79,000, Italy 36,000, and Denmark 28,000 refugees (Morina 1997, page 8). In other words, all foreign countries (with GDPs, on average, 5-7 times the Yugoslav GDP, and populations 15 times the population of Serbia and Montenegro) took care of a little over 700,000 refugees, that is, approximately the same number of refugees the small and poor countries Serbia and Montenegro pro-vided for, where, at the time, around 5,500 war invalids lived.

More precisely, since March 1992 around 180,000 people from the territory of for-mer Socialist Republic of Croatia took refuge in FR Yugoslavia, mainly from the parts of the country controlled by a new – mildly put, nationalistic – regime in the former Yugoslav republic. Another 250,000 refugees are to be added to the above-stated number – people who had to leave the territory of former Republic of Srpska Krajina (Northern Dalmatia, Lika, Kordun, Banija, Eastern and Western Slavonia). Therefore, out of the total number of 800,000 Serbs who had lived in the Socialist Republic of Croatia until 1990, around 400,000 had taken refuge in the FR of Yugoslavia by mid-1995. During the civil war in Bosnia and Herzegovina – 1992-1995 – an additional 300,000 Serbs refuged or were expulsed, among which were several thousand Croatians and Moslems. During the Bosnian war, it needs to be mentioned, Serbs were expulsed from around 15% of the territory of former Bosnia and Herzegovina from several municipalities in which they comprised 95% of the domicile population. It should also be mentioned that Serbs were during this war decimated in the very same territories in Croatia and Bosnia and Herzegovina as during WWII. These territories were struck the most by both the war in WWII and the civil war during the 90's and Serbs had been the ethnical majority in these regions, especially in Croatia, for centuries. Therefore, for the third time in the 20th century, the Serb population in these areas suffered a threat of utter physical extinction (Marinković 1993).

Refugeeism in Serbia and Montenegro has been a mass phenomenon for over a decade. Almost every 10th inhabitant of this country is a refugee, whereas only 570,000 of them have the internationally recognised refugee status, while 100,000 have no status whatsoever. If it be of any comfort, in the period of 1967-1991, there were 171 million people struck by war worldwide, out of which ›only‹ 700,000 lived in industrially developed countries (Farlane A. 2000). Until 1993, there were as many as 40 million refugees registered among them, with a tendency of constant growth (Flatten et al. 2001). The growth in the number of refugees worldwide resulted in a growing number of researches investigating the refugee issue (Dyregrov K., Dyregrov A., Raundalen M. 2000).

According to the official sources (Čavić 2000; Ilić 2001), the overall number of refugees in Serbia and Montenegro at the beginning of the 3rd millennium amounts to nearly a million, compared to the present 200,000 ones in Croatia. Sociologist Ilić V. (2001) maintains that there are around 800,000 officially registered refugees, while the remaining 200,000 appear as the so-called grey figure. Excluding nearly 200,000 refugees expulsed from Kosovo during 1999, all the refugees living in this country belong to the category of the so-called »extremely traumatised«, as mentioned by Becker (1997), paraphrasing the author of this expression, much better known Bruno Bettelheim for whom »extremely traumatised« implies, beside long exposure to stress, the fact that the trauma is deeply personal, that it is of social, that is, human origin, and last but most importantly, that it involves the experience of possibility of the loss of one's own life. It should be stated that, in terms of this population, refugeeism, beside combat experience at the front lines, belongs to the most intensive stressful experiences (Kaličanin, Bjelogrlić, Petković 1992).

The experiences of sudden and major changes in life are difficult to overcome – unpleasant and painful ones even more – which was confirmed by many authors (Peretz, Kaminer 1991; Becker 1997, Priebe, Bolze, Rudolf 1994). Traumatic experiences, in their narrower sense, remain more present in sensory than in symbolic memory, making intimate traumatic experiences difficult to verbalise, that is, to translate into the language of communication. Trauma therefore continues to »live«, not only in subjective life of an individual, but, according to some authors (Farlane A. 2000), keeps on transferring from generation to generation as a heritage of collective experience.

Refugees from Croatia and Bosnia and Herzegovina were coming to Serbia and Montenegro in three major waves. It is interesting to note that the first-wave refugees from Croatia and Slovenia (until April 1992) had had higher living standards prior to the war conflicts than the domicile population of Serbia who received them. Besides, there were more accommodation capacities in the FR of Yugoslavia at the time, and solidarity of the citizens of Serbia and Montenegro was more prominent. On the other hand, the second-wave refugees (from 1992 until mid-1995), as well as the third-wave ones (august 1995, mainly from Croatia) had already had lower living standards than the domicile population, or managed to take only a minimum of their assets when leaving their homes due to war operations of the Croatian army supported by NATO forces. Therefore, when they arrived in Serbia and Montenegro, they had significantly less resources than the domicile population. On the other hand, the reserves of the population that received them had in the meantime been exhausted, while the majority of capacities of refugee camps in Serbia had already been filled, which additionally aggravated the already serious situation.

The distribution of refugees in Serbia (Jovanović Z. 1994) was such that Belgrade received as much as 36.8%, Central Serbia 25%, and Vojvodina 37%, while an insignificant part was sent to Kosovo. It should be noted that according to the current Law on Refugees of the Republic of Serbia, passed on April 1, 1992, every expulsed person is to lose his refugee status if refusing the accommodation provided by the state (Filipović 1996). The fact that the Milošević regime took no systematic care of refugees is supported by the following data: refugees, prior to their expulsion, had had employment in 80% cases – when becoming refugees, only 10% of them had regular employment (Milosavljević 1997).

There is no doubt that the first-wave refugees were warmly welcomed by the domicile population of Serbia, especially by their relatives and friends, whose natural and spontaneous reaction was to lend a supportive hand to their nearest in their misfortune. However, neither refugees nor those who offered their generous support could foresee that their refuge status would last that long, which created, and still creates even today, a whole range of specific problems and phenomena which deserve the attention of researchers dealing with massive disasters. These refer less to the aspect of forcible change of living conditions than to the forced adjustment to the new living conditions. More precisely, these phenomena are related to conflicts within the population of refugees and the expulsed, and their conflict with the domicile population, even with those who offered them immediate help.

In 1993, 42.6% of the total refugee population were children (Rudić et al. 1994). The majority of them experienced the loss of a family member and changed several places of residence during their refugeeism. These children were also exposed to long-term separation from their fathers (who were mainly at the front-lines) and short-term separation from their mothers (involved in solving existential and material problems of their families).

The whole population of refugees was, doubtlessly, exposed to an external destructive impact. Two thirds of refugee families in Yugoslavia were even separated – a part lived in various refugee conditions, while the other part remained in Croatia or Bosnia (Milosavljević 1994). One research (Popov, Mitrović, Stokić 1994) showed that those the most often absent from the remaining family were the father or one child. 10.5% of these families remained in war zones, 21% in their previous place of residence, while as many as 26% were transferred from one accommodation centre to another. Conflicts in such families grew significantly – from 29% prior to their refugeeism to 60% following their becoming refugees. Refugee families living in collective accommodation centres (around 20%) show a lower degree, in terms of statistical significance, of manifestation of closeness among their members, as well as a significantly lower degree of the need to be active, with increased rigidity, more precisely speaking, a decreased ability of adjustment to the new living conditions.

The mortality rate among refugees is today almost ten times the rate of the remaining population of Serbia (the same rate in which it is also increased) – 10% of the refugee population die annually, out of which, as much as 2% commit suicide (cf. magazine ›Humanist‹, published by Red Cross, Belgrade, July 1998). The suicide rate among them is nowadays 60 times the rate of suicide prior to their refugeeism (it was around 15, now it amounts to 1,000 per 100,000 people). The previously quoted datum that 90% of the refugees found family accommodation is more than dubious since it leads to the conclusion that refugees live with other families. The truth is that their number is decreasing and providing for their own accommodation is more and more present. The state and humanitarian organisations do not provide for a slightest part of their living costs, making their rather scarce money reserves thaw at a dramatic pace since the main part of their assets (real estates, furniture, livestock, means of production), the total value of which amounted to between 10 and 25 billion US dollars, remained in Croatia (›Humanist‹, 1998, page 12) and Bosnia. The position of refugees is further burdened by the fact that half of the expulsed population (those from the former Republic of Srpska Krajina, that is, the Republic of Croatia) have limited political rights, primarily concerning the right to vote. Even if they have the right to vote, they cannot truly exercise it, due to objective reasons. Full restoration of these rights raises the issue of the actual possibility or their exercise (Aldetarro 1997).

Besides, the tendency of decrease in refugee aid, provided for the refugees from Croatia and Bosnia and Herzegovina by the Yugoslav Government and the international community, was becoming more and more evident. Foreign refugee aid dropped by 49% during 1996 only, and was realised mainly in the form of victuals and medicine supplies (Ranković 1997).

Certain researches (Aćimović 1998) showed that there were also problems related to the subjective acceptance of refugees by the majority of the domicile population of Yugoslavia. The above-mentioned research proved that no significant resistance towards refugees was present but also showed a lack of deeper and more organised psychological and social support. The government, as well as a good portion of the population, takes the position of understanding and compassion only declaratively while expressing ambivalence in concrete situations.

Emotional and psychopathological response of refugees

As already described (WHO 1992), the emotional reaction of those struck by a disaster undergoes a certain regularity and successiveness. During the first couple of days, the most frequent reaction is paralysing passiveness and-or maladaptive fear. The first phase is followed by the so-called emotional reaction marked by anxiety, nightmares and compulsive memories (flash-backs) related to details or the traumatic experience on the whole. The signs of PTSD may also appear during these usual reactions. The response to a peacetime accident is similar to what has been previously described, except that in this case an experience of interior emptiness may first appear, followed by, after a longer period of time, processing of the traumatic event in the form of asking questions about the deceased, possibly accompanied by the appearance of fear, guilt and anger, and ending in overcoming the situation and turning towards the future (Schüffel 1989).

People involved in providing refugee support and accommodation in Serbia (Vlajković 1997), noticed that the most present mental reactions were crammed by fear and depressiveness. It was also found out, in similar situations but different settings (Raphael, Lundin, Weisaeth 1989; Hendin, Haas 1984), that depressive and anxiety feelings were also prevailing, although some other symptoms were also recorded. Observing psychical responses of refugees in Serbia, Desimirović (1997) notices several phases in their reaction: 1. an emotional shock and disbelief phase, in which a negation of unbearable reality appears as the basic element of keeping mental

17

balance, immediately followed by 2. the phase of using mental defences, most often those of dissociative character (separating emotions from motor actions, separating parts of reality in general, separating time from space, and the like) or relying upon repression, and sometimes even possessive and compulsive mechanisms of defence. The reality becomes acceptable not earlier than in the third phase. We would like to add one more phase to the phases described by Desimirović, the so-called phase of presentiment or warning, as described by Lazarus (1996) in his classification of phases. The phase was, according to our experience (out-patient department work with refugees treated due to their trauma-provoked neurotic problems), observed in refugees in Serbia as a pre-phase to the three phases described by Desimirović. It is characterised by a hunger for information, attempts of gaining control over emotions, refusal to think of the objective threat of danger and minimising the problem significance. It should also be noted that Desimirović noticed in the third phase a phenomenon observed in concentration camps in WWII: identification with the aggressor (justification of crimes committed against the Serb population by the enemy).

On the basis of his extensive experience with refugees from the Republic of Croatia in 1991–92, Vlajković J. (1997) describes four phases of refugee behaviour: 1. euphoria phase (described, typically, by the following words: »Finally, we are safe«), 2. sadness phase (with depressive mood in a whole range of varieties, characterised by the hunger for information, need for protection and escape, and very interestingly, a special relation towards family photographs), 3. protest phase (expressed against everyone, mostly against the persons in charge of providing refugee aid, as well as against the people who received them in their homes, followed by breaking ties with relatives, changing place of residence and the like), and, finally, 4. constructive confrontation with the situation phase, characterised by seeking alternative solutions to their problem (employment, emigration, seeking ways to return to their old homeland) or resigned acceptance of the situation and deepening dependence on others.

Certain Serbian authors (Srna J. 1997) noticed that refugees who suffered from flagrant violence had a prolonged period of recovery, making another phase, the so-called emotional instability phase, appear following the depressive one and prior to the already mentioned protest phase (characterised by anger, wrath...). Violence, as an illicit, immoral and excessive use of force, causing damage both to others and, indirectly, to oneself, causes in refugees shock and disbelief at first (most often not visible), with so-called traumatic psychological infantilism (regressions of various depth).

There are at least three specificities related to violence committed against the Serb population in the civil war in former Yugoslavia. Firstly, victims of torture were, in the majority of cases, descendants of Nazi concentration camp victims or WWII ethnical cleansing victims while the crimes during the civil war were most often committed by the descendants of WWII war criminals (i.e. Ustashas – members of the Nazi army of Croatia in WWII). Very importantly, the majority of them was very well known by the Serb population. Jovanović A. (1997) even found, in his extensive research into the impact of war mental trauma on the family, that several victims imprisoned in concentration camps during the civil war had also been imprisoned by Nazi Croatian forces during WWII. The second specificity of violence committed against Serbs during the civil war was, as reported by several authors (Petrović, et al, 1994; Jovanović 1997), the bizarreness and numerousness of the methods of torture. The third feature of this sort of violence was directed at humiliating the victims. Jovanović (1997) determined and described as many as 41 ways of physical torture, 12 mental methods, and 27 combined – physical and mental – forms of torture. Respecting both your and our own need for a distance from violence, we will not list the forms of torture in this paper. Petrović, et al. (1994) write that, when discussing the issue of torture, mental torture (committed over 141 subjects locked up in Croatian prisons) was aimed at attaining the so-called »3D syndrome« (debility, dependency and dread), with the ultimate aim of creating an ethnically cleansed territory mainly inhabited by the Serb population or of assimilating victims – terrified Serbs –, the process of which involved, more or less directly, the so-called brain-washing procedure.

One of the researches (Jovanović A., Pejović M., Marinković J., Dunjić D., Aleksandrić B., Nad I.1996), on the basis of the GAF (Global Assessment of Functions Scale) value, determined that refugees scored significantly lower values on the scale in comparison to the domicile population, both at war and in non-war zones.

It should be emphasised that, referring to the World Health Organisation (1992) estimates, 20% (or around 4 million) of the total refugee population of the entire former SFR Yugoslavia, developed PTSD, implying that around 800,000 persons from the above-mentioned region developed PTSD. The most affected were, as usual, children aged 12 and under, for whom the risk of PTSD development was four times the risk of the remaining population. Another 200,000 people who developed PTSD in peace time, that is, while living in regions not directly affected by war operations, should be added to the above number.

The percentage of people with PTSD among those who took refuge in Serbia and Montenegro was around 25%, which was observed in similar situations in other settings – for example among the Moslem population during the same war (22% refugees from Bosnia and Herzegovina in Netherlands developed PTSD (Drozdek 1997), or during disasters in peacetime (22% as a result of the airplane crash in Ramstein, Germany in 1988 – Jatzko H., Jatzko S., Seidlitz H. 1995).

Aleksandar Jovanović research (1997) showed that the subjects who developed PTSD (unlike the people with similar or the same features) had urban backgrounds, had been of unfavourable economic status prior to the outbreak of the civil war (the average income per family member being lower than 100 DEM per month), that

19

among them there had been significantly more of those (65% : 35%) who had suffered torture solely for being of Serb nationality. It should be emphasised that the experimental and the control group in this research were equal in terms of presence of ethnically mixed marriages and that the variable did not differentiate those who mentally decompensate, which needs to be emphasised since certain authors (Popović 1994) are of the opinion that ethnically mixed marriages' members develop mental problems more often. The research conducted by Jovanović (1997) also showed that there were significantly more present mental illnesses (schizophrenia and psychotic depression), prior to, as well as following, the torture, in the families of subjects with PTSD. Among the group of subjects who developed PTSD, there were significantly more (as a psychiatric co-morbidity) personality disorders, alcoholism, psychosomatic illnesses and drug addictions determined. The same research, involving 160 subjects (80 with and 80 without PTSD) who had been equally exposed to war stress and exposed to torture to the same degree (35 in experimental and 35 in control group), showed that the subjects with family heritage of mental illness, as well as those who scored lower values on the Family Homogeneity Index, significantly more often developed mental illness.

The researches targeting children (Rudić et al. 1994) showed that the refugees who were mothers were often depressive (riveted to TV sets in their expectation of the latest news, without ability to meet emotional and other needs of their children in such a state), while the refugee children in refugee camps showed more mental disorders (fearfulness and depressiveness) in comparison to those in the so-called family accommodation. Elder children showed higher sensitivity and behaviour disorders, school children showed ill manners, adolescents early-age alcohol and nicotine addiction. Besides children, the elderly are especially affected. As already stated in the above-text, higher mortality rates were recorded among them, as well as various forms of less recognisable depressiveness.

As of the raping of Serb women by Croats and Moslems, rapes were committed most probably by all three sides in the conflict, amounting to around 2,000 cases in all, as stated by Jakulić and Krstić (1994). However, only the Serbs were generally and globally spoken of as the perpetrators of such crimes. The above authors wrote that all raped women, who, of course, had sought professional help (we should remind of the »grey« statistical data related to all sides in the conflict, including rapes committed by the UN soldiers deployed to the region), were diagnosed with disorders such as PTSD (mainly with flash-backs and nightmares), or Acute Stress Reaction. Those psychiatrists maintain that the so-called systematic rape (at the command of military officers), allegedly committed by all sides in the conflict, is nonsense. Ten women described by Jakulić and Krstić were imprisoned in Moslem concentration camps and raped; they conceived and consequently developed mental diseases. They were treated at Belgrade's psychiatric hospital »Dr. Laza Lazarević«.

The Serbs who lived in diaspora were also exposed to negative influence of war stress through the media's satanisation of Serbs and through their identification with the suffering of close relatives and the nation as a whole. A research (Vukas 1994) carried out in Sweden showed that a decrease of neurotic responses (primarily tension and fear) was observed in Serbs of the first and second generation living in that country. In over 50% of out-patient department cases of Serb emigrants, a significant increase of depressiveness, metabolic, cardiovascular and gastrointestinal diseases was observed. It was also observed that young subjects and Serbs married to Swedes, and interestingly, to Croats and Moslems, seemed to have been protected from such illnesses. As of the mixed marriages, the children must have played a »buffer«, i.e. a mediator role in mitigating ethnic conflict potentially destructive to a mixed marriage. The most affecting stress factor in these subjects was the experience of being jeopardised at war (for example, betrayal committed by friends, etc.), the experience of manipulation of the media outside Serbia, more than the front-line experiences and drafting and, finally, the refugee situation. In relation to the former Yugoslavia war conflicts, Serbs working abroad obviously felt the most deeply the events that could jeopardise, beside other things, their own existence – that being the aggravation of the international position of the country of their origin, which included the possibility of employment loss, even expulsion from the country they lived and worked in.

Instead of a conclusion

It is a fact that many aspects of refugee life remain unknown, due to several reasons. First of all there is the shame many refugees feel to talk about their problems at all, then comes the fear of not being understood, and the fact that not an insignificant number of them (children especially) are prone to consciously keeping negative feelings under control, shunning to burden their nearest or those that could help them with their problems. There is also an argument that a reaction to disaster lasts, this way or another, around two years (Schüffel 1989), and many refugees failed to change their status for years. The list of the problems related to refugeeism problems research should be completed by the fact that society was caught unprepared for the refugee catastrophe, whatever be the nature of that unpreparedness. In our case, it is related to health care organisation and insufficient support both by the international community and by neighbouring countries. To the above-stated problems we should add the lack of cooperation of some experts, the non-existence of a timely and general national plan for disaster management, and the like.

There is no doubt that the so-called background factor also influenced the magnitude of refugee disaster in Serbia (Raphael, Lundin, Weisaeth 1989). The factor is related to the war conflicts that were seething in its nearest vicinity, and – what is more – in the very regions, especially in Croatia, in which Serbs comprised the majority of the population. All this resulted in the fact that present refugees had the traditional family, regional and local experience of WWII disaster. The whole region involved in the 90's war conflicts had been occupied by the Nazi Independent State of Croatia during WWII, thus sensitising the large number of its population to refugee exodus. The latter factor, recognisable as a paranoid attitude of the major part of population towards Serbs, was also registered by authors from Croatia (Klain, Vidović 1992) similar to factors observed, for example, by Von Bayer-Kattee (1995) in relation to the former GDR regime and political opponents of communism.

As shown by experiences of other authors investigating similar situations (for example in analysis of mental disorders of Vietnam soldiers – Fontana, Rosenheck, Horvath 1997 or of German peace-keeping soldiers deployed to Bosnia - Schunk, Shade, Schüffel 1998), a very important factor of prevalence, and, of course, treatment of such problems is the group cohesion of people under stress threat, the group that, in such a situation, can evolve into a self-help group. As emphasised by German authors, social and professional homogeneity of the group plays a very important role. In the case of refugees in Serbia and Montenegro, this role is played by family cohesion, better maintained in conditions of family than collective accommodation.

As of the support, it should be stated that refugees absolutely needed it in every possible way – primarily, as material support (food, clothing, footwear and the like, a sort of support bearing a certain psychological significance), then, as informational support (in a social and cognitive sense, in the form of providing explanations of current situations and available mechanisms of coping with problems), and finally, as emotional support (clearly verbalised and repeated demonstration of respect, understanding and emotional feedback).

As of providing psychological support to refugees, it needs to be stated that its direct aim is the affective relief of refugees and to direct them at current vital issues, while the indirect one is the prevention of more serious mental disorders in refugees (WHO, 1992).

Counselling, the most frequently used form of such refugee support in Serbia and Montenegro, was carried out in all psychiatric institutions, almost all health care institutions in the country, and refugee camps (visited by health care teams comprising either psychiatrists or psychologists, or both). Counselling was, like elsewhere in the world, performed in combination with medicamentous therapy (anxiolytics, antidepressants), most often individually (face-to-face with the person seeking help) (Vlajković 1997), then, as counselling of key persons, i.e. persons functioning as the relay of mental health and mental infection, and finally, as group counselling, most often when a smaller or larger group of people spontaneously formed. These groups not seldom evolved to either self-help groups, that is, psychotherapeutic groups without professional presence (Mitrović et al. 1994). As some other psychotherapists

22

(Milivojević 1998), we ourselves (Opalić, Džamonja, Nikolić, Barišić-Rojnić 1997) had good experience in the application of group psychotherapy to groups comprised of local population and refugees with serious mental disorders.

Psychological or psychotherapeutic aid to adolescents and women implied a knowledge of the specific nature of refugeeism, but also the ability to meet concrete needs of adolescent and female refugees, as reported by J. Srna (1997), in reference to both other therapists as well as her own experiences in providing such help. Srna emphasises that meeting refugees' needs to be understood at once and on the spot and encouragement must never be disregarded.

Confronting the past (Mitscherlich), as a remedy to continue life in gloomy reality, is, of course, possible as a spontaneous process in refugees. However, as reported by Van der Veer (1995), when such process is supported by professionals, they (the professionals) must not disregard that providing information and early confrontation with reality has a key role while diagnosing the disorder itself is in the background. The traumatised is primarily encouraged in the free expression of negative feelings and memories. The person providing support must be sensitive to both individual differences between the suffering and specificities of their culture and tradition. In relation to this, an adequate approach was applied – an Orthodox Christian cultural framework of psychological counselling when Serbs are concerned (Alečković-Nikolić 1998) or a modification of the well-known approaches (as a tolerance of being late or not attending the scheduled counselling) when the Balkan nations in general are concerned (Schumacher 1995).

As well as in peacetime accidents, it was necessary to recognise patients that could possibly develop PTSD over time, while the seriousness of possible somatic injury and the duration of their being exposed to psychic stress was of key importance, as already observed in relation to traffic accidents (Winter 1996) and in soldiers on the other side of the front in the former Yugoslavia war conflict (Hećimović, Supek-Ilić, Kulović 1992). A significant predictive value for a subsequent development of PTSD had the symptom of depressiveness and aggressiveness immediately following the trauma (Jovanović, Pejović, Vranić, Radotić 1997). Similarly, this is also valid for children and elder refugees (Weine et al. 1998).

Let us draw a conclusion. Since the beginning of the war conflict in former Yugoslavia, refugees who took refuge in Serbia and Montenegro were mainly Serbs, with a minor number of members of other nations, mainly from mixed marriages. The refugees mainly originate from the areas of former Yugoslavia predominantly inhabited by a Serb population, excluding the first wave of refugees from Croatia and Slovenia.

Refugees that arrived in Serbia mainly provided for their own accommodation or were supported by their families/friends (without the support of the Government) while only 5% were sent to the so-called refugee camps, which later on proved to be by far the most unfavourable way of taking care of them. Beside living in refugee

23

camps, the factor of age, namely, for the elder and children, proved to be a high-risk factor in terms of developing mental disorders, then the refugees that had had mental problems before, as well as those expulsed with a family history of mental illness, and, finally, the refugees that were imprisoned in Moslem or Croatian concentration camps only due to their Serb ethnicity.

Serbia and Montenegro pursued the refugee policy to a great extent conditioned by the unfavourable policy of great powers and the degree of its own (dis)organisation in the situation of solving a range of serious social problems caused by the semi-warlike state and total economic, cultural and media blockade of society. Humanitarian organisations were dosing their refugee aid mainly in accordance with their government policies, which was insufficient and significantly less than the aid they provided to other former Yugoslav republics.

Summing up the results of solving overall refugee issues in Serbia, it could be stated that they reflected the destiny of the whole country, which, in the meantime, had disintegrated. Unprepared for the exodus (by which they were saving their bare lives), refugees in Serbia were warmly received, albeit in a disorganised manner. Therefore the Government transmitted the majority of the burden related to solving their issues more or less to the very population, and then to the very refugees. A planned and organised network of counselling centres was also missing, which was stated by the health care authorities of the then FR Yugoslavia (Mitrović, Popov, Vlajković, Krstić 1994). Plans related to solving and possibly researching refugee problems made afterwards mainly remained unaccomplished plans. They were also related to researching and solving conflicts within refugee families, or conflicts between refugees and their relatives, or members of the families that received them. Specifically, the hopes of all participants in refugee drama were not met, as their expectations from each other were unrealistic. All sides disregarded that the most responsible for refugee disaster were public officials of the countries they had to escape from and leaders of those communities that received them, but most of all, world powers which seem to be the most responsible for the outcomes of the unenviable destiny of refugees.

Resume

During the war conflicts in the Western Balkans from 1991 to 1995, nearly a million people were expulsed from their centuries-old homelands in Croatia, Bosnia and Herzegovina and other parts of former Yugoslavia. Those who took refuge in Serbia and Montenegro were provided with health care, scanty aid in food and almost no political rights.

Ninety-five percent of refugees found their shelter in so-called family accommodation – at their friends and relatives' homes, and, increasingly, in rented houses and apartments (20-40%), while 5% were placed at refugee camps which proved to be by far the most unfavourable solution for them (disaster subculture and the like).

Earlier research showed that the risk of mental decompensation in refugees was several times the risk in domicile population, while around 25% of refugees developed Post-traumatic Stress Disorder and other reactive mental disorders. Refugee families were both mentally and economically more imperilled than other families. The part of refugee population which is the most exposed to risk are former psychiatric patients and their family members, then children, the elderly and, especially, those with the experience of home loss or family member loss during the war conflicts.

As of their reaction to refugeeism, according to the majority of authors, refugees, on average, reacted in the first phase in an upset manner, in general shock, then in the second phase by outstanding hunger for information, protesting aggressively, and developing various illnesses in the third phase.

Besides, the risk of secondary (subsequent) and tertiary (extending to several generations) traumatisation in this population and in families providing support to them is very high.

Foreign countries and NGOs outside Serbia responded to refugee problems almost indifferently, Serbia itself did so in an unprepared and disorganised manner.

2. About the (Psycho)Pathology of Somatically Traumatised Subjects in a Trauma Context

When we speak about psychological aspects of somatic diseases, we must state that they do not concern the usual reactions to disease coloured by mild neurotic disturbances, first of all anxiety, which is by itself mobilising and motivates the patient to recognise the signals and needs of his own body. It is not a question of reaction to physical trauma either, when at the very beginning the patient is confused, after which anxiety develops, with possible avoidance behaviour, or even depressive reaction (the latter with poor prognosis) and only later on the traumatic experience rationally integrates into the life of the injured, without psychological sequelae. We are speaking about the psychological mechanism assumed to be the basis of the development of somatic disease (Rudolf 2000).

In trauma, a reaction occurs as a consequence of the summation of influence by several factors: the effect of outer pressure, loss of an object or overpowering of the ego by the excessive effect of stimuli, depending on the theoretical angle from which we look at traumatisation. In the psychopathological sense, trauma may produce a sequence of subjective disturbances (disorders of emotional response, blackouts, lowered self-esteem, interpersonal problems, change in the value system of the injured, and it may also lead to distorted experience of the person immediately responsible for trauma - the perpetrator or criminal in the sense of trying to justify his actions towards the injured as victim (Peltzer 1995).

Physical handicap caused by trauma in many ways interferes with the issue of personality identity, more exactly, the experience of body scheme on one hand, and the feeling of the so-called body ego on the other (Marković, Jovanović, Vranić 1994). Body scheme, however, implies cognitive knowledge of body parts, while body ego concerns subjective experience which may correspond to the body scheme or not. The first is more related to the neuropsychological basis of body functioning and the second to physical identity. The body scheme is formed in the tertiary zone of the cerebral core, that is, in the lower parietal and temporooccipital lobe (in Broc's zones 21. 37, 39 and 40). It is founded in the sensorimotor experience in which the human being *via* outer tactile and inner cenesthetic stimuli becomes conscious of his body part, most easily and most commonly *via* motor movements of the body. In experiencing body ego, on the other hand, a more representative component of body experience participates in which emotional and cognitive components are equally present as sensory components.

In other words, body identity is related to the total development of existence in certain time and space. For that reason, sociologists (Papić 1992) rightfully point out that the body is not a mere natural phenomenon, and that nature is created in human environment. According to them, it is closely related to the role of the body in the profession of the patients, in their complete life style (e.g. the profession of the physical worker or recreational or professional sport), in their dressing style (not only gender-specific, but specific for the dominating style, fashion), in the human attitude towards the exterior appearance of the body (through make-up, use of cosmetics or by active body shaping, such as jogging, body-building, aerobics, and similar activities).

Recognition of those psychosocial factors is present in the so-called »disease concept« (Scheer 1989) of what is in the conscience of the somatically ill thought to be essential in the occurrence of the disease. This is valid, first of all, for younger patients, especially those under 60 years of age. The relation of the psychological to the physical aspect of the human existence, which is related to the social and cultural and may be recognised in the language as well, is confirmed; for example, in our language we say: »My heart aches« (when sorrow or painful longing for something lost is expressed), »To fall in« (in the sense of »to adjust«), »bear on one's back« (not a physical but a responsibility burden) or, to mention a phrase in German: »Was kränkt, macht krank« (»What insults causes illness«), etc.

Thus, we live in a society in which consciousness and will are still idolised (as initiative enforcement, enforcement of the fighting will and competition). On the other hand, we are overrun by general social, economic and moral crises (the global blockade of society, the bombing of the country, enormous pauperisation, that is, stratification of society, perturbation of moral values, etc.), the general consequence of which is the limitation of individual will, which produces an increase in general tension, one of a psychological nature, as well. And this cannot but be recognised in the functioning of our organs, including those for moving.

Studies of the direct presence of the psychological factor in the development of most somatic diseases with patients hospitalised due to internal medical diseases (Künsebeck, Lempa, Freyberger 1984) indicated that as many as 41% of patients manifest recognisable psychological disturbances, first of all, anxiety and depression. A similar study, this time exclusively on surgical patients (Vijay, Shamsundar, Shivaprakash, Sripram 1988), indicated that 45% of the patients treated as outpatients have various psychiatric symptoms. For this reason it is imperative, almost urgent, to learn all psychosomatic aspects of acute diseases, which, without doubt, include physical injuries. Among those, a special problem is presented by patients with amputations, whose degree of traumatisation is catastrophic in quality and quantity. The reason for this lies in the fact that amputation is associated with the experience of life threat to the patient, intensive psychological and physical pain, and permanent professional and social disability (which, again, affects the change in experiencing body scheme, social role, and the patient himself).

It should be pointed out that patients with somatic diseases »do not like«, that is, avoid anything related to the word »psycho«, to psychiatry, and especially to diagnosis with that prefix, experiencing them more or less as degrading. Unfortunately, physician somatists have a similar attitude. Willert and Wetzel-Willert (1991) report that during diagnosis, treatment and their relation toward the patients, only 20% of physicians accept the aforementioned »psychosomatic« reasoning.

The importance of the psychological background of somatic diseases is indicated by the experience of somatic physicians (Bischoff, Zenz 1989), which state that even in the most developed European countries, in up to 40-80% of cases, patients seek medical advice only when body symptoms occur, and even then they do not take them seriously but continue to ask advice from their neighbours, friends and pharmacists, and we may add (especially in our situation), again with some other physician of the same speciality. This is because the therapist, in spite of his professional expertise, does not create the right, that is, psychotherapeutic relation with the somatically affected patients, or, as the aforementioned authors say, because they do not respect the patient's theory of the disease, his own opinion on the reasons why he became ill, since, as our patients say, »the physician does not listen to him enough«. What is almost as important is that the physician did not make a connection between the patient's theory on the disease and his own professional opinion, which includes as much as medical and social assumption of his profession, which is often forgotten. The latter, namely, implies automatic overtaking of the patient's social role by the affected (we think, first of all, on accepting professional advice), which does not have to be the case, of course.

The results of one catamnestic study with patients treated for body injury (see Laer 1991) indicate the importance of psychosomatic exploration of orthopaedic diseases, where as much as 40-80% of operations were not necessary since they did not achieve the results because of which they were undertaken. This expert sees the reason for this, among else, in the out-of-date definition of disease, which does not accept that injury may also have a protective function in the psychological life of an individual, and in the psychological structure of the surgeon who, as he writes, »suffers« from the obsession referred to as »life-saving syndrome« or »helper syndrome«. Namely, they consider the diseases as something absolutely bad, and as such, the surgeons think they should be dealt with as soon as possible with all available resources and removed from the existence of those who come for help. In another words, intervention should be made so that the physicians themselves could be relieved.

Psychosomatics, let us conclude, fill the empty space between objective findings of the physician and subjective experience of the patient, which in medicine could be extremely large« (Ahrens, Hasenbring 1991).

Any offered type of explanation of the nature or structural relation between the psychological life of an individual and occurrence of body diseases in a narrower sense includes emotions as an unavoidable mediator (Adamović 1983), and according

to some theories (Petronijević, 1998; Rudolf, 2000), as the crown of the total psychological life of a human being. Namely, emotions do not exclusively contain the emotional basis of one's conception of oneself and the world, especially not only feeling
related to the exterior and interior body stimuli, but what we call the content of our
total self, existence project, that is, the total attitude of the diseased towards the world
(Bernal, 1984; Opalić, 1988). Feelings, in other words, significantly mark the content
which concerns human environment, culture and religion, that is, which concerns the
total social and spiritual being of the affected. The inclusion of emotions in body
functioning can be seen even in the anatomic human structures, in the nervous system
of the organism, through the work of older brain regions in the so called limbic system
and thalamus, those, as the word goes, human »doors of the consciousness«, and especially the hypothalamic, the pituitary and complete system of glands with interior
secretion. Emotions are the theoretical and empirical key substance of the bio-
psychological-social model for explaining psychosomatic diseases. The explanation of
fear and aggression occupies a special place among them.

Affects related to individual diseases of the muscle apparatus and loco-motor system, then some personality traits (problems with aggressiveness first of all), as well as
relatively complicated family situations of the patients (aggressive and dominating
father, for example). From the 1970s onwards, surgeons have tended to interpret mus-
cular disorders as expressions of intrapersonal conflict and failure of some »neurotic«
defence mechanisms with which the individual, exaggerated in some of them, maintains his own personal balance (Noble, Roudebush, Price 1952).

The psychogenic component of certain diseases imposed itself in the practice of
surgery *post festum*, as well, most frequently after unsuccessful interventions. Thus
Laer (1991) found in 1,973 patients with fractures of juvenile bone cysts that surgery
does not significantly influence disease recurrence. The same is the case with problems of the fibullo-tibial tendon (302 patients), where the same author found prolonged gate instability, independent of whether the intervention was conventional or
surgical.

When speaking of a depressive trait in somatic patients, a more recent study
(Cashman, Dijkers 1990) indicated that depression in patients operated on due to
spinal cord injury is the only statistically significant psychopathological feature. Interestingly, depression in patients who had undergone surgery was significantly higher in
staff perceptions than perceived by the patients themselves.

Another study (Jäckel et al. 1989), with instruments which mainly concerned the
general health condition, indicated that there was no essential difference in the evaluation of the psychological status of patients by the staff and by the patients themselves.
Also, in patients with discus prolapse (Ahrens and Hasenbring 1991) a significant
presence of depression (insomnia, loss of appetite, sexual disorders) was found using
Beck Depression Inventory. Judging by the examples given by these two authors,

related to patients with discus hernia, it is obvious that some personality traits increase the probability of a depressive reaction in this category of orthopaedic patients. It is a case of an unconscious need for adaptation to the surroundings at any cost, as well as a habit to be at service to everybody on all occasions. The authors are of the opinion that behind this lies a passive confrontation of the diseased with their surroundings.

As to personality traits of patients injured in traffic accidents, several studies have indicated specific personality traits in more than 50% of subjects. Those injured in traffic accidents are described as impulsive, risk-prone, as well as those who have problems with authorities, as latent aggressive, that is, potentially suicidal, as prone to self-injury, persons with permanent feeling of guilt, etc. Nevertheless, some investigators (Barbel 1998) have found that patients injured in traffic accidents are psychopathologically the least different from healthy subjects. It is not difficult, of course, to reach the conclusion that the registration of traits in those who caused a traffic accident is influenced by a series of factors. Among them is lower intelligence (Lasko, Orr, Pitman 1989). The indirect influence of social parameters of the injured should also be taken into account, among them the fact that most of them are younger people and that they come from industrial, that is, workers' environments.

Finally, psychopathological changes in surgical patients may be so apparent that they are manifested as recognisable psychiatric entities. The study of Kuhn et al. (1988) with instruments such as BSI (Brief Symptom Inventory) and SMARTS (Short Michigen Alcoholism Screening Test) indicated that out of 101 patients with leg bone fractures, as many as 73% patients belonged to the group of patients with a psychiatric diagnosis, although psychiatric consultation was asked for only 6% of them. Out of those one half belonged to alcoholism, 38% to personality disorders, 21% to neurosis and the same number to dystimic disorders.

More frequent diagnosis, and even psychosis (in relation to healthy subjects) was confirmed in injured patients treated after traffic accidents (Jin, Araki, Wu, Zhang, Yokohama 1991; Winter, 1996). It is very probable that the psychological status of those injured in traffic accidents is equally the cause of injury, that is, the cause of the traffic accident, and its consequence. A similarly psychopathological reaction, as well as the explanation, is seen in war participants, where in a considerable number it was confirmed that in 30% body injury (and general exposure to war stress) is a significant factor for the occurrence of Post Traumatic Stress Disorder and that the incidence of PTSD is positively correlated with the duration and intensity of combat exposure (Buydens-Branchey, Noumair, Branchey 1990). Hećimović, Supek-Ilić and Kulović (1992) registered significant presence, as they said, »of psychosomatic regression« (gastric ulcer, infections and similar) in patients who survived more intensive trauma.

As a negative emotional experience, stress is associated with biochemical, physiological, cognitive and behavioural changes, directed in two ways, either to the change of stress experience or adaptation to the effects it causes (Berger 1997). There is no doubt that stress, more or less directly, is in correlation with psychosomatic disorders. Thus, Nyberg, Frommberger and Berger (1998) as an obligatory co-morbidity pathology of Post Traumatic Stress Disorder after body trauma, beside depression, alcoholism and phobias, mention psychosomatic diseases, first of all pain syndromes. Similar observations in a similar population were reported by Feinsten and Dolan (1991).

These phenomena actually concern life events which became an unavoidable research subject related to stress, trauma, that is, life crisis, long ago. Thus, the positive correlation between the so-called accidental physical injury and the number of life events 6 months prior to the injury (Whitlock, Stoll, Rekhdahl 1977).

The aforementioned is thus more clear when we have in mind that successful coping with stress implies, beside the use of reduction mechanism for the exterior threat and direction toward emotional stability, the development of adequate relations to other persons. Optimistic patients, as well as those with expressed self-esteem, that is, with a strong ego, recover much faster after body injury and surgery (Taylor 1995). Stress reaction to body injury, as any reaction to stress, indicates from the dynamic view a certain process structure (Jovanović, Pejović, Vranić, Radotić 1997). Inhibitory phase or a period of dumbness, that is shock, occurs immediately after stress, followed by a depressive phase or balancing with possible suicidal behaviour (especially in cases of severe body injury with disability), finally to end with the phase of reintegration or rational stress reaction.

When surgical diseases are treated in the hospital, hospitalisation itself is also a stress provocation. In this situation, beside the pain and massive body dysfunction, separation from the family, insufficient information about the condition and uncertain outcome of treatment are also stressogenic. Medical interventions also have their effect, especially those of invasive aggressive character, such as surgery with anaesthesia.

In one study of hospitalised surgical patients (Vögele, Steptö 1986), depressive condition was confirmed in 24-38% of cases. When we speak about fear of surgery, we should indicate that it contains several components (fear of the loss of control during surgery, the patient's fear that he will not wake up after surgery, then fear of suffocation during anaesthesia, fear of pain, scars or functional organ damage after the intervention. However, it must be pointed out that anticipatory postoperative anxiety, that is, worry (the so-called »work of worrying«, according to Janis, 1958 in Berger 1997) has a positive effect on postoperative recovery. Namely, as extreme fear before operation inhibits rational processes, thus in the background of very low preoperative fear is a neurotic mechanism of denial, which, each in its own way, interfere with rational concept and application of basic information on the disease.

In conclusion, we have found in literature (Vlajković 1992) as many as eight strategies of coping with stress consequences in Yugoslavia. The first of them is confrontation and implies the immediate and energetic effort to change the stressful situation to one's own benefit. The second strategy represents the search for social support, either emotional, such as receiving encouragement, or cognitive, in the sense of finding new information. The third strategy is reduced to the planning of long-term coping with the stressful situation, which includes problem solutions of various aspects of stress for a longer period. The fourth concerns the strengthening of inner self control, and the fifth, distancing oneself from the stress situation. The sixth and seventh strategy are mainly cognitive and are related to finding a positive meaning of stress for the affected. The last strategy of psychological coping with stress consequences is avoidance and flight from the stressful situation and is recommended for coping with short-lasting stressful events and quick effects of negative consequences of stress. All mentioned strategies begin with the known question: »Who knows why it is good that this happened to me?«, and end with the decision to accept the responsibility for the stress situation.

Everybody agrees that the consequences of social isolation after stressful experience are harmful for the injured. Social engagement or social support to the injured is, as we know, commonly provided by the partner – relatives and friends can also be helpful, and, finally, in the psychological sense, the closer and wider community, and even pets. Social support is especially important for removing the effects of high-intensity stress. Care should be taken here that provision of support is not intrusive, i.e. that it should be provided by the right person and at the right time. The support provided must be in accordance with the needs of the injured and does not help much, as many have noticed, in the case of great material loss or when it is offered at a time when the injured does not expect it.

It should be said that in Yugoslavia the most frequent techniques for coping with stress are brief counselling techniques. In addition, a series of other methods is used and they always include various techniques of muscle relaxation (autogenic training, guided fantasies, exposition *in sensu* and *in vivo,* transcendental meditation, yoga exercises, and similar methods). Hypnotherapy is not excluded as well as alternative medicine, especially in the situations of massive tragedies (Petković 1994).

For removing psychological consequences in patients who underwent amputation, a specific technique, otherwise rarely used, of behaviour therapy has been applied in Yugoslavia – the desensitisation of experiences during artificially stimulated rapid eye movements (Eye Movement Desensitisation and Reprocessing - EMDR). The authors (Jovanović, Pejović, Vranić and Radotić 1997) stated that it gave quick positive effects.

In patients with evidently severe somatic injuries and disabilities of various degrees, we apply a more complex procedure to remove possible psychological disorders. We use the following methods (Opalić 1990, 2000): individual and group psychotherapy (psychoanalytic, existentialist, and of other orientations), family therapy (mainly of systemic provenance), and a series of social interventions for the benefit of the injured, such as individual help of social workers from institutions where the patient is treated or from the social service in the place of his residence.

In the psychotherapy of psychosomatic patients in the narrower sense, in Yugoslavia we apply all techniques for removing the consequences of stress (Uexküll 1996). However, it seems that body-directed psychotherapeutic methods are most commonly used (progressive muscle relaxation or behavioural method of conditioning), as well as some methods of group therapy, including self-help groups (therapeutic groups without the presence of a professional) which have the advantage that they are cost-effective and free of the harmful effects of potential labelling of people with psychological problems when they turn to professionals in institutions for help. In addition, group therapy for patients with physical trauma is often more efficient than individual therapy. It absorbs aggression and despair more quickly, stimulates emotional reaction as well as mass projections of the traumatised, and causes the psychological problem of the injured to surface more easily and thus to be dealt with more efficiently.

Sometimes psychological changes of people with somatic injuries in Yugoslavia require subsequent psychiatric hospital treatment (Jovanović, Pejović, Vranić, Radotić 1997). This is the case when the injured tried to commit suicide or had more than obvious suicidal ideas, when the patient encounters extreme misunderstanding in the family or is in conflict with aggressive member of the family, that is, in situations when the surgical patient becomes an alcoholic in the pretoxic or chronic phase and, finally, when clinical presentation indicates the signs of aggressive, that is, homicidal behaviour, and hospitalisation temporarily protects the surroundings.

Family therapy with close relatives of the injured should prevent secondary traumatisation of the family members (traumatisation due to consequences of injury to a family member). It is expected to re-establish a network of family relations broken by trauma and to recognise the dysfunctional family ways of communication. It helps the patients to overcome the conflict between two realities, traumatic, war or outside the family on the one hand, and posttraumatic, peacetime or family reality on the other (Jovanović 1997).

Medication therapy is applied exclusively as adjunct, that is, *ad hoc* therapy for reducing mainly anxious and depressive symptoms including those of somatoform character, primarily, pains (Kaličanin, Bjelogrlić, Petković 1992). Good results with antidepressants (tricyclic antidepressants, MAO-inhibitors, and serotonin uptake inhibitors) have been achieved in the therapy of psychological disorders of the injured by Nyberg, Frommberger, Berger (1998). Fast effects in similar situations are also achieved with sedatives (diazepam, bromazepam) which cure temporary anxious reactions, and we ourselves have had good experience with injured patients without indications for psychotherapy.

To conclude: Therapeutic interventions directed to treat the symptoms of psychopathological reaction of the somatically traumatised and other surgical patients start as early as in the phase of diagnosing the psychological status of the injured, that is already at the moment when simulation is distinguished from hypochondria, that is masked depression and conversion from somatic disorder. This is important to avoid unnecessary hospitalisation and even more unnecessary surgery as well as to refer the patients to adequate psychotherapeutic, group therapeutic, and other psychiatric methods of treatment.

Resume

This paper presents in its general outline arguments of theoretic reason in general medicine and in the psychology of somatically diseased or injured individuals (interdependence of somatic and mental, which is recognised in the dynamics of somatic disease or injury development, in the relationship physician-patient, as well as in subjective phenomena accompanying somatic injury and especially hospitalisation).The role of stress, i.e. the neuro-physiological, behavioural and psychodynamic theoretic framework of interpretations of organism and certain organs reaction to illness as a stress.

The correlation between illness on one side and a series of mental factors related to development and personality features of the diseased or injured person on the other, was explained within three dominant theoretic approaches in psychosomatics, i.e., within psychoanalysis in its narrower sense. Emphasising the neglected psychotherapy attitude towards the diseased in the clinical work with somatically injured and diseased individuals, positive experiences provided by such an attitude in their treatment were presented.

II

Studies of Dreams of Traumatised Subjects

1. Dreams and Trauma

The picturesque, emotion-sated and, most of all, succinct method in which they express the current existential position of their subjects makes dreams a valuable source for the recognition of possible psychological problems of traumatised persons. As the »imperial path to the unconscious« (Freud 1948), as the »harbinger of existence« (Boss, 1975), or a »reserve-driving fuel of existence« (Stojanović 1999), dreams, undoubtedly, broaden the field of knowledge about humans, human nature in general, and especially about the individual hidden side of human life, which suffering due to of physical injury certainly belongs to.

Before we present dreams in a kind of systematic overview, and subsequently in their phenomenal plane, i.e. as reported by their dreamers, it is necessary to state two things about dream research. The first is that dream research has a qualitative character, which partly also includes the explanation of their therapeutic role in coping with the traumatisation effects. The second is that this research has focused on the interpretation of relations among certain traits of dreams on the one hand, and of traumatisation characteristics, including the overall social climate in which they occur, on the other.

As to the overall framework of issues related to the significance of dreams in trauma research, it is certainly necessary to say that dreams are an expression of a complex process of integration of daily experiences and their informative value as to the subjective state of a dreamer cannot be denied. Although there are researchers (Globus 1991) who claim, based on the results of their studies, that the content of our dreams is quite random, whereas only what we remember of our dreams has any sense, researchers agree, concerning the relation between dreams and trauma, that the relationship between them and the dream content is indisputable and very indicative. More precisely, dreams in which one can recognise the contact of the dreamer with previously experienced trauma are useful. They serve to process unpleasant emotions related to trauma. In contrast, dreams in which the contact cannot be recognised or is even prevented are more or less useless, almost harmful (Cartwright 1991; Hartman 1991). In the first case, as Freud noticed in his time, dreams are a result of replay compulsion, whose purpose is to free the dreamer of negative feelings caused by the traumatic experience (Popović 1999). True, here one could ask to what extent the replay of trauma in dreams is a useless continuation of traumatic experience and to what extent it is desirable coping with the traumatic experience. The latter, it seems, is true mostly for so-called exclusive dreams which do not require any special interpretation but rather need to be listened to, since they are fraught with negative emotions (fear, first of all) so that the mere physical presence of a listener and the sharing of negative experiences with the dreamer have a therapeutic effect. It is necessary to say that the presence of dreams in psychotherapy is usually a sign of an increase in the affective tolerance of the dreamer (Trijsburg 1989), that is, a forewarning of the dreamer's exit from a deep depression (Opalić 1999). In this sense, dreams undoubtedly have a so-called traumatolytic, or emotionally detoxifying, function.

Several researchers (Levin et al. 1991; Esposito et al. 1999; Schreuder 1995) point out a high correlation between the dreaming of dreams coloured with fear and other negative emotions on the one hand, and the replay of the traumatic (war, exile, etc.) experience on the other. It was also confirmed that having dreams with contents related to the experience of being jeopardised (Cartwright 1991; Stepansky et al. 1999) is related to trauma, especially immediately following a traumatic event (Hartman 1990). Truly, this type of relation depends on an array of factors, the general adaptation of subjects being among them, so that the better adapted less often have dreams related to traumatic events (Peretz, Kaminer 1991). It requires no special emphasis that the so-called nightmares and the dreams colourfully termed »night terrors« directly replay a traumatic event, exactly as does night fear in children (pavor nocturnus). There, the prevalent unpleasant emotion (the experience of menace, threat, feeling of humiliation, experience of destruction, etc.) has the function of recontextualization of the threat that the dreamer has indeed experienced in trauma. Traumas themselves can come from childhood, from the subject's immediate past or present. They can be predominantly somatic, as in our case, or predominantly mental. Then, they can be (Biesold 2000) short-lasting (Type I) - such as auto accidents, technological and natural disasters and criminal violence; or long-lasting (Type II) - such as the refugee situation, life in a war prison, child abuse, various persecutions, etc. Disasters or accidents, classified generally into natural (earthquakes, floods, droughts, and so on) and humanitarian (man-induced such as war, Holocaust, political torture, refugees, rapes) may also concern, as some authors rightly point out (Barett 1996), so-called normal life (chiefly mental traumas related to bereavement, significant changes in living conditions, etc.).

Nightmares are actually compulsive memories of trauma, paroxysmal traumatic hypermnesias, that is, psychological scenes of trauma memories in dreams, diminishing the symbolic function of dreams and, as observed by many researchers, invariably repetitive. In other words, the repetitiveness of nightmares results from their occurrence in the non-REM dream phase, unlike symbolic dreams which occur during the REM phase of sleep (Schreuder 1995).

However, recurrent dreams are not the only trauma-related dreams. Dreams whose content is death and dying, then dreams without any trauma content in the phenomenal sense but which are simply repetitive (so-called »serial dreams«), then many dreams concerning relationships among people, are also trauma-related. In a broader sense, the phenomena referred to as parasomnias, including sleep-walking, sleep talking and insomnia in general, are also trauma-related, in addition to nightmares and night terrors (Self-help Line 1999). Similarly this is true for so-called sadness dreams, fear dreams, but also for so-called anticipatory dreams and premonitory dreams (Kimball 1985).

Resume

Dreams, as »the imperial path to the unconsciousness« or »the harbinger of existence« have for a long time been unavoidable material of mental life research, especially the one not directly accessible.

Dream research, to a great extent, depends on the theoretic framework used in their interpretations. However, the majority of theoretic approaches imply the knowledge of life history, present mental state and current preoccupations of the dreamer involved.

As for the trauma itself, it almost unavoidably affects the contents of dreaming, most often in the form of repetition of dreams with unpleasant emotions related to trauma (fear, experience of being jeopardised, dreams with contents related to dying, etc.). The appearance of »nightmares« and dreams with recurrent contents, i.e. compulsive dreaming of trauma in the form of the so-called dream series which are believed to have therapeutic effect (so-called emotional de-toxication related to traumatic contents), is also related to trauma experience. Traumatised subjects less often have dreams of symbolic character.

Research of dreams of traumatised people is increasing globally, since traumas of various origins are also on the increase.

2. Research of Dreams of Refugees

Introductory remarks

Research of dreams, more present in literature in the past (Schmitz 1978), have always attracted those involved in the research of human mental structure of various motives. Whatever the case may be, the research is characterised by several features, independent of the aim and subject of the research. First of all, dreams are, basically speaking, of qualitative character, even when quantitative statistical procedures are obviously involved. The fact is that combined approaches to dream research – quantitative (statistical) and qualitative (accounts of dreams followed by their interpretation) ones – are rather rare (Urbina S. 1981). Another important feature of the research of dreams is the prior declaration of theoretic paradigm used for the investigations. As of this research, to state it here, the theoretic approach involved is an existential-analytical one (Boss 1985, Opalić 2000), the principles of which are to be presented, e.g. illustrated, in further text. Other features of the research of dreams depend primarily on the aims of the research and subjects themselves.

Bearing in mind that nightmare dreams or night terrors, pavour nocturnus in children and repetitive dreams (i.e. dream series), as well as dreams the contents of which are death or dying, are generally more trauma-related, it would be expected that these types and contents of dreams are more present in the refugee population. Refugeeism is a typical long-term trauma, that is, a so-called humanitarian trauma (Barret 1996)

Subject of the research

The main subject of this research is related to features of dreams of a specific population under stress – in other words, mental state and dreams of the chronically traumatised refugees from former Republic of Srpska Krajina (Lika, Banija, Kordun and Western Slavonia) expulsed from their homeland in 1995, as well as a dozen of refugees from Kosovo and Metohija expulsed in 1999. The main focus of this paper is the correlation between certain, primarily socio-demographic and, to a certain extent, psychopathological features of subjects on one side, and the contents and types of their dreams on the other.

More particularly, this paper investigates the dreams of 109 subjects living in a provisory refugee camp on the outskirts of Belgrade, in Krnjača, situated between the road to Pančevo and the Danube. Accommodation conditions in the camp are more than unfavourable – the camp consists of old workers' huts, in which the whole families live in single, cramped rooms with double beds, sharing with others primitive sanitary and hygiene systems (troughs, privies, etc.). Čavić (2000) states that the majority of refugees in refugee camps in Serbia and Montenegro live in similar conditions.

Aims of the research

Generally speaking, our subjects – refugees – have been living under chronic stress for several years, making it, therefore, the main aim of this research to achieve a more complex, that is, qualitatively better insight into their mental, i.e. psychopathological state several years following their expulsion. The aim is to be attained by quantitative analyses of various features of their dreams, qualitative and unconscious phenomena of one's mental life.

Aims of the research in a more narrow sense are as follows:

1. Insight into the manner of dreaming and certain formal features of dreams, i.e. proneness to dreaming and taking into consideration refugees' dreams,
2. More complex insight into the phenomenology of dreaming, i.e. into the contents of dreams in a wider sense,
3. Grasping the emotional tone of dreams as their essential feature,
4. Differentiated insight into the types of dreams related to certain psychopathological states (primarily neuroticism), as well as certain aspects of the personalities of refugees (introversion and the like),
5. Determining the correlation between the contents of dreams, that is, dream types on one side and certain parameters of the psychopathological state (neuroticism or proneness to PTSD reaction) on the other,
6. Determining significance of correlation between the frequency of dreaming and types of dreams on one side, and certain relevant features of mental state of subjects (family cohesiveness and features of activities in coping with trauma) on the other,
7. Determining possible differences in dream types and contents of dreams between refugees on one, and non-refugee population (somatically traumatised and subjects with no trauma experience whatsoever) on the other side.

Research method

a) Research sample

The narrower sample (experimental group) was comprised of 109 refugees from the above-explained refugee camp. The remaining part of the sample (control group) was comprised of non-refugees, 175 of them, out of whom 105 denied any trauma experience whatsoever, while 70 were recently traumatised subjects from Belgrade.

Table No. 1 shows socio-demographic features of the whole sample of refugees and non-refugees. As of the socio-demographic features, no statistically significant differences were discovered in relation to the sex, age and marital status of refugees and non-refugees.

Table No. 1 : Socio-demographic features of refugees (N=109) and non-refugees (N=75)

SOCIO-DEMOGRAPHIC FEATURE	SUBJECTS	REFUGEES (Experimental group)		NON-REFUGEES (Control group)		TOTAL	
		f	%	f	%	f	%
Sex	Male	56	51.4	95	54.3	151	53.17
	Female	53	48.6	80	45.7	133	46.83
Age	20 years and younger	11	10.1	16	9.1	27	9.51
	21-30 years	23	21.1	39	22.3	62	21.83
	31-50 years	34	31.2	76	93.4	110	38.73
	50 years and over	41	37.6	44	25.2	85	29.93
Marital status	Married	73	67.0	88	50.3	161	56.69
	Not married	36	33.0	87	49.7	123	43.31
Education	Elementary	21	19.3	13	7.4	34	11.97
	Secondary	70	64.2	66	37.7	136	47.89
	College & university degree	18	16.5	59	33.7	77	27.11
	Undeclared	0	0.0	37	21.1	37	13.03

b) Classification of dreams

Classification of the dependent variable, i.e., dream features, was performed, as in our earlier research of similar character (Opalić 2000), on the basis of the original classification. In doing so, we, expectably, relied on the similar classifications of dreams by other authors, most of all the classification given by Kimball (Kimball 1985) and »Self-help Line« (1999), London. The former consists of 6 dream types, and the following types were taken from this classification: anticipatory dreams (we called them prophetic dreams), fear dreams, and sadness dreams (we did not include into our classification the dreams related to drug abuse, so-called dreams dreamt as a gift and premonitory dreams). Of the latter, the Self-help Line classification, which is more contemporary and comprises as much as 16 types, we took the following: collective dreams, death dreams, decision-making dreams, ESP dreams, cure dreams, health-related dreams, sexual dreams, human relations dreams, nightmares and dream series. So-called lucid dreams (similar to the decision-making dreams and prophetic dreams), past-life dreams and some other dream types were not taken from this classification. To the above-chosen types, we added the following: group dreams, psychotic dreams, dreams related to family, dreams related to work, dreams related to trauma in general, and finally, dreams related to the old homeland.

The following features were added to formal features of dreams in our classification: extensiveness of dream description (short, moderately extensive and very extensive), presence or absence of dream commentary, the number of dreams described (one, to, three or more), time of dreaming (present, recent past, childhood), time dreamt in the dream (presence, recent past, childhood), as well as emotional tone of the dream (without emotion, pleasant emotions, unpleasant emotions, unpleasant feelings causing the dreamer to wake up, fear in dream, and depressiveness in dream).

c) Research instruments

Beside the above-mentioned socio-demographic data acquired from the appropriate questionnaire, all subjects were asked to fill in the following psychometric instruments: PTSD-10 Scale (investigates the presence of PTSD symptoms), Impact of Events Scale (determining active or passive attitude in coping with accident effects), Brief Eysenck's Personality Inventory (investigating the presence of neuroticism and extroversion presence), as well as Family Homogeneity Index (determining the degree of family cohesiveness of subjects).

The subjects were, in the end, given a blank sheet, with the following request: »*Please describe one or more of the dreams you remember and state in which period of your life you had it/them*«.

No instructions were given to the subjects, except that some of the subjects who hastily replied that they did not dream or could not remember their dreams were urged to remember one and describe it.

d) Statistical data processing

On the basis of the offered classification we evaluated and entered into the protocol the values of the presence of features of every subject's dreams.

Statistical data processing followed – the first step involved the determination of quantitative values (frequency and percentage) of certain features and dream types, i.e. certain formal features of dreaming in the refugee group (experimental group) and in the group of somatically traumatised and non-traumatised (control group). Percentages of certain features were determined in relation to the total number of refugees (109) and the total number of non-refugees (175). The next step was to mutually compare three groups of subjects: refugees (109), somatically traumatised (70) and those without any experience of trauma whatsoever (105).

Statistical significances of differences between the presence of a certain dream feature in the refugee group were then calculated, as well as the presence of the same feature in the group of non-refugees. Pearson's χ^2 test was used for determining the statistical significance of differences between the presence of a certain dream feature in the investigated groups, with the application of Yates correction.

The last step involved the determination of the statistical significance of correlation between certain dream features and dream types on one side, and neuroticism features (neuroticism score according to the Eysenck's Brief Personality Inventory and PTSD-10 Scale score), then a family cohesiveness test (total values on FHI), as well as the values of passive and active attitudes in coping with trauma (on the Impact of Events Scale) on the other side. This step was performed by the linear correlation test within the group of refugee subjects only.

Research results

a) Phenomenology of dreaming and dream types of refugees

The values of frequencies and percentages of dream features, i.e. the reaction of refugees when asked about their dreams, are presented in Table No. 2.

Table No. 2: Values (frequencies and percentages) of the answers to the question related to description of dreams of refugees and non-refugees

REACTION TO THE QUESTION RELATED TO DREAM DESCRIPTION		SUBJECTS					
		Refugees		Non-refugees		Total	
		f	%	f	%	f	%
Without dream description	Blank sheet returned	1	0.9	70	40.0	71	25.0
	"I don't dream"	1	0.9	16	9.1	17	6.0
	"I don't remember my dreams"	14	12.8	13	7.4	27	9.5
	Total	16	13.6	99	56.5	115	40.5
With dream description		93	86.4	76	43.5	169	59.5
TOTAL		109	100.0	175	100.0	284	100

As presented in the above table, absolute figures show that the refugees returned a blank sheet significantly more rarely ($\chi^2 = 52.65$; p<0.01, F= 1), while at the same

44

time giving, in a statistical sense, significantly fewer (χ^2 = 9.36; p<0.01, F= 1) replies »I don't dream«.

A significant difference between the investigated groups in terms of the reply »I don't remember my dreams« was not determined.

The following Table No. 3 shows the overall phenomenology of refugee dreams in relation to non-refugee dreams.

Table No. 3: Values (percentages and frequency) of individually-taken features of dreams of refugees (N = 109) and dreams of non-refugees (N = 175)

DREAM FEATURES		SUBJECTS					
		Refugees (109)		Non-refugees (175)		Total (284)	
Broader	Narrower	f	%	f	%	f	%
Extensiveness of dream description	Short	26	23.9	22	12.6	48	16.9
	Moderately extensive	44	40.4	42	24.00	86	30.3
	Very extensive	21	19.3	12	6.9	33	11.6
With commentary about the dream		25	22.9	12	6.9	37	13.0
Number of described dreams	One	20	18.3	46	26.3	66	23.2
	Two	6	5.5	8	4.6	14	4.9
	Three and more	65	59.6	20	11.4	85	29.9
When did you dream the mentioned dream	Childhood	8	7.3	12	6.9	20	7.0
	Recent past	80	73.4	25	14.3	105	37.0
	Present	14	12.8	42	24.0	56	19.7
To which period of your life did the dream refer to	Childhood	2	1.8	13	7.4	15	5.3
	Recent past	63	57.8	21	12.0	84	29.6
	Present	32	29.4	42	24.0	74	26.1
Emotional tone of the dream	No emotions	7	6.4	2	1.1	9	3.2
	Pleasant emotions	35	32.1	30	17.1	65	22.9
	Unpleasant emotions	52	47.7	36	20.6	88	31.0
	Unpleasant emotions that wake you up	12	11.0	17	9.7	29	10.2
	Fear in dream	40	36.7	32	30.6	72	25.4
	Depressiveness in dream	24	22.0	18	10.3	42	14.8
Dream-types	Psychotic in a narrow sense	3	2.8	3	1.7	6	2.1
	Group dream in general	9	8.3	22	12.6	31	10.9
	Group dream about family	27	24.8	19	10.9	46	16.2
	Dream about war	44	40.4	17	9.7	61	21.5
	Dream of desire fulfilment	35	32.1	35	20.0	70	24.6
	Dream about old homeland	45	41.3	13	7.4	58	20.4
	Dream recurrence (serial dreams)	56	21.4	31	17.7	87	30.6
	Dream about trauma in general	47	43.1	23	13.1	70	24.6
	Dream about physical trauma	1	0.9	12	6.9	13	4.6
	Prophetic dream	5	4.6	9	5.1	14	4.9
	Collective dream	0	0.0	14	8.0	14	5.4
	Decision-making dream	1	0.9	1	0.6	2	0.7
	Dream of healing-hint	2	1.8	8	4.6	10	3.5
	Dream about relations with other people	22	20.2	41	23.4	63	22.2
	Dream with sexual contents	3	2.8	5	2.8	8	2.8
	Dream about death	16	14.7	14	8.0	30	10.6
	Dream with ESP	0	0	0	0	0	0
	Dream with health-related problems	0	0	8	4.6	8	2.8

45

As presented in the above Table No. 3, differences in replies (more obvious in percentages due to the unequal number of subjects in each sub-sample) are clear.

By calculating the statistical significance of differences between dream features present in both basic groups (refugees – non-refugees) and in three sub-groups (refugees – somatically traumatised – non-traumatised or with mental trauma), we arrived at a more relevant insight into differences between narrower features of dreams, that is, dreaming. The following Table No. 4 shows those dream features that are present statistically differently in investigated groups.

Table No. 4: Formal dream features significantly, in statistical sense, differently presented in two basic groups, a well as in three sub-groups of subjects (with χ^2 values, level of statistical significance of differences checked by Yates correction application and Freedom degree)

DIFFERENCE TO THE ADVANTAGE OF	FORMAL DREAM FEATURES	PARAMETER VALUES OF STATISTICAL SIGNIFICANCE OF DIFFERENCES IN THE PRESENCE OF CERTAIN DREAM FEATURE BETWEEN THE GROUP OF REFUGEES (109) AND THE GROUP OF NON-REFUGEES (284)			PARAMETER VALUES OF STATISTICAL SIGNIFICANCE OF DIFFERENCES IN THE PRESENCE OF CERTAIN DREAM FEATURE BETWEEN THE GROUP OF REFUGEES (109), SOMATICALLY TRAUMATISED NON-REFUGEES (70) AND NON-TRAUMATISED NON-REFUGEES (105)		
		χ^2	p (with Yates correction)	Freedom degrees	χ^2	p (with Yates correction)	Freedom degrees
Refugees	Very extensive description	8.90	0.0029	1	10.40	0.0055	2
	Description of dreams with comment	13.94	0.0002	1	16.34	0.0003	2
	Three or more dreams described	72.14	0.0000	1	76.24	0.0000	2
	Dreams dreamt in recent past	98.18	0.0000	1	101.11	0.0000	2
	Contents of dreams dreamt in recent past	65.45	0.0000	1	67.93	0.0000	2
Non-refugees in general	Dreams dreamt in present	4.60	0.0320	1			
Non-traumatised non-refugees	Dreams with contents related to childhood				9.07	0.0107	2

The following Table No. 5 shows the results of statistical analysis of determining differences in the presence of emotional and typological features of dreams between the previously-stated groups (also in two ways in relation to the statistical significance calculation).

46

Table No. 5: Emotional features and dram types significantly differently present, in statistical sense, in two basic groups, a well as in three sub-groups of subjects (with χ^2 values, level of statistical significance of differences checked by Yates correction application and Freedom degree)

DIFFERENCE TO THE ADVANTAGE OF	EMOTIONAL OR TYPOLOGICAL FEATURE	PARAMETER VALUES OF STATISTICAL SIGNIFICANCE OF DIFFERENCES IN THE PRESENCE OF CERTAIN DREAM FEATURE BETWEEN THE GROUP OF REFUGEES (109) AND THE GROUP OF NON-REFUGEES (284)			PARAMETER VALUES OF STATISTICAL SIGNIFICANCE OF DIFFERENCES IN THE PRESENCE OF CERTAIN DREAM FEATURE BETWEEN THE GROUP OF REFUGEES (109), SOMATICALLY TRAUMATISED NON-REFUGEES (70) AND NON-TRAUMATISED NON-REFUGEES (105)		
		χ^2	p (with Yates correction)	Freedom degrees	χ^2	p (with Yates correction)	Freedom degrees
Refugees	Unpleasant emotions	21.87	0.0000	1	27.69	0.0000	2
	Fear in dream	11.08	0.0009	1	12.04	0.0024	2
	Depressive contents in dream	6.44	0.0112	1	9.27	0.0097	2
	War in dream	35.62	0.0000	1	38.10	0.0000	2
	Recurrent dream	40.24	0.0000	1	44.61	0.0000	2
	Dream related to trauma	28.00	0.0000	1	30.01	0.0000	2
	Dream about family	8.58	0.0034	1	10.03	0.0061	2
	Dream about old homeland	45.31	0.0000	1	47.86	0.0000	2
Somatically traumatized non-refugees	Dream related to somatic trauma	4.15	0.0416	1	20.16	0.0000	2
Non-traumatised non-refugees	Dream with collective symbols	8.91	0.0028	1	23.62	0.0000	2
	Dream about relations with other people				12.93	0.0016	2

b) Correlations between having dreams of a certain type or feature and psychopathological, i.e., mental status of refugees

The following Table No. 6 shows the results of calculating correlations between certain features and dream types on one side, and neuroticism, general proneness to PTSD symptoms reaction, family cohesiveness and the manners of refugees' reacting to trauma on the other.

47

Table No. 6: Statistically significant correlations (with values of significance levels) between certain dream features and total value on the neuroticism scale (according to Eysenck), PTSD-10 Scale score, FHI Test results and Impact of Events Scale scores of refugees

DREAM FEATURES	SCORE VALUES ATTAINED ON CORRESPONDING INSTRUMENTS				
	Total PTSP-10 Scale	Eysenck Personality Inventory neuroticism values	Total FHI score	Impact of Events Scale values	
				Active attitude	Passive attitude
Very extensive description of dreams	r =-0.16 p =0.047				
Three or more dreams described		r =-0.18 p =0.030			
Fear in dream					r =0.17 p =0.033
Depressive contents in dream			r =0.19 p =0.025		
Group dream		r =0.22 p =0.010			
Dream about family	r =-0.19 p =0.023				
Dream about trauma in general				r =0.16 p =0.049	
Dream about death			r =0.22 p =0.019		

Examples of dreams of refugees placed at a refugee camp

The below text will present those refugee dreams that in a succinct and vivid manner illustrate the results of quantitative analyses of aspects of dreaming related to its form and contents.

For the sake of a more systematic review, we shall first of all present the most frequent, i.e. dreams that in a most undisguised manner reflect the trauma pain (days of expulsion, war or the atmosphere of refugees' lives in their old homeland immediately before expulsion, first days of refugee life etc.)

Unfortunately, much more uncommon are the refugee dreams with symbolic character, hiding enigmatically possible explanations of the reasons of their refugee life. The very refugee situation is indirectly recognisable in these dreams, as psychoanalysts would say, through the dream-work. This group comprises the dreams the contents of which are universally human.

a) Dreams with trauma from the period of expulsion or pre-expulsion torture

Description of a 66-year-old elementary school teacher from Kordun who has been living in a refugee camp for 9 years. She writes about the refugee trauma which happened to her once again after 50 years:

»All my dreams are related to the past war events, to people I used to know, especially my pupils. I dream them, but I also dream my sons, especially the younger one currently living in another town. The memories in my dreams often bring me back to 1941, when I, still a child, became a refugee for the first time. I dream of the village where I was born, the one that I lost during the war, my friends, my pupils. Such dreams wake me up very often and trigger in me fears for the future of my beloved ones«.

Similar to the above in their saturation with the experience of pain, loss and nostalgia are the dreams of a 55-year-old worker, a refugee from Western Slavonia:

»I constantly dream of the dead, my mother and my father. I talk to them. I dream of my colleagues in Kutina, my workplace before our expulsion. The Croats mistreat me on the ethnical basis, they curse my Serb mother. I also dream that I am returning to my homeland.«

The following are the dreams of a 59-year-old widow from Lika with a 10-year refugee experience, who lost her husband to the last war conflict. Prophetic interpretation of dreams, so present in the folk interpretation of dreams, pervades the contents of her dreams and her comment:

»I dreamt my most fearful dream, I remember clearly, on September 20, 1991. In my dream Franjo Tuđjman, in person, has come to arrest me. I resist him. I have a gun with me and I want to kill him. Then, in the dream, a thought crosses my mind: »But, I am not a murderer«. I wake up. After 6 days only, Paragas' Usthasas come to burn down my village, the most wonderful in the world, to massacre the people. Ustashas killed everyone they found in their houses«.
»The second dream I dreamt 26 months ago. It was so fearful. Dark sky spreads over our Serbia and the hail is hitting us from up there. As it turned out later on, the hail were Clinton's bombs«.
»The third dream I had only a week ago. It resembles the first one I described. They are arresting and expelling the Serb population«.

How prophetic the dreams of this misfortunate refugee are is left to the readers to decide.

A 60-year-old refugee from Kordun briefly describes the dreams related to pre-refugee trauma, during the Croatian purge of Serbs in the summer of 1995, in the area mainly inhabited by a Serb population.

»I dream of bombing, columns of refugees in Serb exodus on August 8, 1995 near Dvor. Dead bodies and injured men lie all around. This dream keeps on recurring«.

A 34-year-old woman, a refugee from Kosovo, unemployed, married, without children, describes her dreams:

»Almost every night, but not every single one, dusk appears in my dreams. I am in my street in the town where I was born and used to live. I am standing in front of my house which I cannot enter but want to so much.
I dream of the dead bodies of my nearest, I dream of decaying bodies.
I dream of Albanians chasing us. We are hiding in secret places only I know of, and we manage to escape the tragedy«.

A dream of a 22-year-old man from Lika summarises the essence of the previously described dreams – the dreamer is obviously overflowed with traumas and recurrent dreams that still have not performed a »detoxication« of the subjective world of the dreamer. The dream is described as follows:

»I constantly dream about war, slaughtering, torture, murders, rape, in short, the destruction of us – the Serbs. I dream about my house in flames – it is burned down«.

b) Dreams with contents related to refugee life

In this section we shell present the dreams which are often a combination of processing of the trauma situation caused by expulsion and newly created refugeeism, or just the latter, being a cumulation of the trauma.

A 59-year-old woman, who has been living in a refugee camp for the past 11 years with her husband and their children, describes her dreams as follows:

»I dream that I am visiting my home and the things that we left there when expulsed. The dream always ends in the same way: police forces of the country I was expelled from are arresting me. Then I wake up and cannot sleep until the morning.
I don't know about the others, but I will go mad in this camp, in this cramped room –

this is where we sleep, this is where we keep our shoes, detergent, dirty laundry… I needn't explain any further.«

Dreams of a 71-year-old woman, who suffered no loss of family members, »only« the loss of her property (which is not a common case), writes:

»I keep on dreaming that I am packing my things, putting them on the car and taking them off. The people surrounding me are all strangers. Nobody is helping me. I am crying. It wakes me up. Then I dream about my house and putting everything in order. Then I am in my garden, sowing lettuce and onion. Then I dream about my water mill. When I wake up, I see nothing of everything I dream about, and become nervous. That's what this goddamned destiny of ours is about.«

A 75-year-old man, whose home near Benkovac was burned down, describes his dreams in a similar way:

»Every night I dream that I am in my old homeland. I dream of being on a boat, fishing. I dream that I am ploughing my land. I always dream that one day I will return to my home. I also often dream that I am building myself a new house«.

Here follows the description of a 65-year-old widower, an economist by profession, from Western Slavonia:

»I've been dreaming all my life. When I was younger I dreamt that I was flying like a bird. I have also dreamt about my late father several times. We discuss how to re-build our house, destroyed during the war, we mention getting a credit, and the like. Since the end of the war, I have dreamt of returning to my old homeland, to my house, but my colleagues and acquaintances avoid me. They would not let me in my own house and the premises of the enterprise where I used to work.«

A 52-year-old war military invalid from Eastern Slavonia describes his dreams in the following way:

»I dream about my house, my possessions, all those little things that used to, and still do, mean a lot to me. I dream about the wounded and the killed, destroyed material property, and, worst of all, ruined families, destroyed friendships and kinships.
I cannot return home, although I would like to be buried where I began to walk, where I spent the most wonderful days of my life. To be healthy and to return to my homeland – that's my greatest desire.
In addition to that, I can't help but feel that the war with our neighbours, who were just

51

of a different nationality, people we used to live with in harmony, was so unnecessary.«

c) Dreams processing refugee trauma in a symbolic manner

The dreams processing refugeeism in an indirect manner, through images and symbols that »safeguard« the dream from painful emotions that can interrupt sleep, are rather rare.

A 26-year-old woman, with 10-year experience of living in Krnjača, refugee camp, with her mother and sister, dreams the following:

Dream No. 1 (dreamt five years ago)

»I dream of lying in a bed, here in the camp. The wind is blowing, I can hear the door squeaking. Everything sizzles around me ominously. I can hear the steps of people approaching me. The wind is so forceful that the walls of our hut turn into ice. I lie in my bed and feel nothing but dreadful coldness.«

Dream No. 2 (dreamt three times, first time a year ago)

»I am in a cave. Everything around me is dark. Suddenly I see planks in muddy and dirty water. They are unstable. Long corridors surround me. These plunks frighten me – everything seems unstable. The plunks are moved by the waves of muddy water. The corridors are wide and long, filled with toilets. Everything – corridors, toilets – lie on the plunks, which sway threateningly. I wake up frightened.«

Dream No. 3 (dreamt seven days prior to her participation in the research)

»I am visiting my colleague. Suddenly I feel panic, because my hosts have no food to offer me. Her husband goes out to pick some grass. He is doing it as if it is of no importance what we are going to eat. They behave as if everything was in perfect order. They look at me and seem to be bewildered at my shock. I wake up feeling so.«

A 49-year-old woman with two daughters and a husband, who took refuge in Serbia from Bosnia and Herzegovina (Moslem-Croatian part of Bosnia), describes her dreams in the following way:

»After six months of our refugee life, during the period of which I kept on dreaming about the dead and about graveyards only, I happened to dream of a woman who told me in that dream: ›The dead remained in Bosnia‹.

Three years ago, on the day of St. Marko, I dream of God at a Belgrade graveyard. I tell him that I am angry at him. God replies: »Why?« And I tell him: »Because you gave Sarajevo to the Moslems.«
Three days ago I dreamt of an island on which a brightly white bull appears. Someone tells me in the dream that the bull appears each year on a specific day. I don't know what that could mean«.

The last dream presented in this section is the dream of a 46-year-old man from the former Republic of Srpska Krajina. He has been living in the refugee camp with his wife and four children for 10 years. Such a dream is rarely dreamt by refugees, being related neither to the trauma preceding the expulsion, nor to the grievous refugee life:

Two months ago I dreamt of some sort of a cat. The cat is chasing a mouse. I am trying to defend the mouse and run after the cat to catch it. All of a sudden, we realise that my brother is missing. We all start looking for him but have no clue where he is. I manage to catch the cat, but it's too late, it has already hurt the mouse. In the end, it turns out that the mouse is in fact my brother, that is, the mouse suddenly turns into my brother.«

The so-called »dream work« is easily recognisable in the group of the above-presented dreams. In the first of them, a difficult existential (refugee) situation is hidden behind the phenomenology of dream contents (plunks swaying above muddy troubled water, everything is happening in a cave), while the last dream reveals the family dynamics previously existing in the live of the dreamer – the dream reveals his rivalry with his brother, his consciously unacceptable wish that his brother should disappear, fear for him, or something else. An ultimate interpretation of these dreams would, of course, demand a detailed knowledge of the subjects' biographies, namely, a detailed interview related to the interpretation of the dream contents, as well as a patient exploration of free association of dreamers to the contents of their dreams.

Discussion

The reason for the significantly more frequent participation of refugees in the investigation of dreams (Table No. 2) is probably the fact that there were no somatically traumatised individuals among them, as they (the somatically traumatised) could not describe their dreams in writing due to their injury. On the other hand, refugees were also more motivated than non-refugees to describe their dreams, realising spontaneously their meaning, namely, the importance of »dreaming out« the trauma and the recognition of messages that their dreams offered them.

Observations related to the behaviour of subjects while being tested support the hypothesis that refugees were more motivated to participate in the research (the experience that the community, in a wider sense, was paying attention at them, and most probably, the therapeutic effect of retelling dreams in coping with trauma effects). We (Opalić 2000), as well as a series of other authors (Trijsburg 1989; Peretz, Kaminer 1991; Barrett 1996; Cartwright 1991), have already reported on the traumatic effect of dreams whose contents are related to disaster, stress and the like.

As presented in Table No. 3, refugees described their dreams in a very extensive manner significantly more frequently. They also commented on the described dreams more often and described three and more dreams significantly more frequently.

Also, refugees more often had dreams related to their recent past (past 4-5 years most probably, dreams related to their expulsion), which was confirmed by the statistically significant presence of dreams whose contents are related to their recent past (the beginning of refugee trauma), confirmed by both calculation methods (Table No. 4).

Non-refugees, however, (confirmed in comparison to refugees) significantly more often described their dreams as related to present time (dreams about everyday life and the like). On the other hand, subjects of the whole control group (non-refugees) significantly more often described their dreams related to childhood, which indicates the openness of their mental life to the unconscious aspect of their overall life, unburdened by emotional »poisoning« of recent life events (Table No. 4). The finding points out the importance of experienced expulsion trauma, i.e., facing imposed refugee status, and indicates a huge (probably still non-exhausted) potential of dreams in coping with refugee trauma.

Similar results were obtained by other researchers of dreams in the population of Vietnam veterans (Esposito et al. 1999) as well as with people with accident experience or with the experience of the so-called normal-life trauma (Barrett 1996).

Regarding the emotional tone of dreams, which most directly influences what the interpreters of dreams in psychotherapeutic procedures of a variety of orientations call the ›dream atmosphere‹, we determined that refugees had dreams coloured by unpleasant emotions significantly more often than the both subgroups of non-refugees, i.e. dreams coloured with fear or depressive contents (most often the scenes of beloved ones' deaths, bodies of the killed etc.) (Table No. 5). For the wider population, the percentage of dreams with unpleasant emotions, as confirmed by a research (Stepensky et al. 1998), is significantly lower.

Table No. 5 also shows that refugees, in comparison to non-refugees, »had dreams related to trauma« significantly more often, as well as another dream type which is evidently traumatic, »of war-related contents«. They also had dreams indicating their possible traumatogenous, but also possible neurotic or depressive, even psychotic origin (which can be re-activated by the experience of trauma). These dreams are

»fear dreams«, »dreams with depressive contents« and dreams dominated by »unpleasant emotions«.

The fact that refugee trauma is, as a rule, also family trauma *par excellence* is proved by the fact that refugee dreams related to trauma, in comparison to non-refugee population dreams, are also and always more significantly related to the whole family. In other words, traumatic scenes in refugee dreams serve as »the family stress screen«, as remarkably described by Lansky and Karker (1989) in their dream analyses.

Dreams related to somatic trauma, expectedly, appeared significantly more often in the group of somatically traumatised refugees (Table No. 5), which was confirmed by our earlier research (Opalić 2000). As it turned out, their somatic injury, beside their refugee status, proved to be the major trauma in their lives. Other authors (Hamner 1994; Schenck, Mahowald 1991) determined a significant correlation between the mental disorder symptoms in general (nightmare dreams, for example) on one side, and somatic illness or somatic injury on the other.

Dreams with the potentially most healthful contents, significantly more present in the control group, are »the dreams related to collective symbols«, and »the dreams on human relations«. They, namely, are the main topic of dreams in the subgroup of those who denied any trauma experience in their lives.

We confirmed (Table No. 6) statistically significant (although not considerable) negative correlations between the frequency of dreaming in general (»very extensive description of dreams« and »three and more dreams described«) on one side, and signs of neuroticism (according to Brief Eysenck Personality Inventory and PTSD-10 Scale score) on the other. This key result in the overall research indicates most convincingly the so-called de-toxicating (Popović 1999), or, conditionally speaking, psychotherapeutic function of dreams with unpleasant emotions. Other authors (Trijsburg 1989; Wood et al. 1992, etc.) agree with the above-stated conclusion. Some researches investigating the issue (Esposito et al. 1999; Schreuder, Klejin, Roojmans 2000), however, found significantly more neuroticism in subjects who had more dreams with unpleasant emotions. The reason for this difference in research results most probably lies in the timing of the investigation of traumatised subjects' dreams. Just as the former group of authors, we carried out the research for a longer period of time after the primary traumatisation, while the latter group carried out its research during the period of acute reaction to trauma.

Contrary to the above result, having group dreams is in statistically significant positive correlation with neuroticism (according to Eysenck), which points, although indirectly, to the conclusion that neurotic problems of subjects are related to the estimation of group reactions (involving, most probably, wider social groups) that can coincide with these phenomena.

An interesting finding, conditionally speaking, is the inhibiting function of fear dreams (probably due to its high intensity also present in dreams) in relation to creating an active attitude in coping with trauma effects. Most probably, it is a very intensive fear which »breaks through« the Ego barriers and penetrates the dreaming contents, inhibiting the majority of the so-called salutary potentials of subjects.

Dreams about family are in significantly negative correlation with general symptoms of PTSD (Table No. 6), which indicates the conclusion that dreaming scenes of family life has a positive, not to say, therapeutic function in coping with mental problems resulting from an individual's trauma. This conclusion, however, is not valid when depressive contents of dreams are involved, since they significantly correlate with the FHI score. The reason for such a finding can most probably be found in the high frequency of loss of important family members of subjects during several years of refugee life, making the dreamer associate family or family atmosphere with this loss in life while the attachment to other family members is still very significant.

Probably the most optimistic, and, in a relative sense, the most important result is related to the positive correlation between dreaming trauma in general, and an active attitude in coping with traumatisation effects (Table No. 6), emphasised by the majority of authors investigating the issue (Cartwright 1998; Barret 1996; Biesold 2000; Čavić 2000, etc.)

Conclusions

Having investigated the aspects of form and contents of refugees' dreams mainly from the former Republic of Srpska Krajina who currently lived in a refugee camp near Belgrade, and compared them to non-refugees from Belgrade, we arrived at the following conclusions:

- Refugees dreamed significantly more often, describing their dreams more and more extensively;
- Refugees significantly more often had dreams related to their recent past than dreams with immediate trauma contents, war dreams, dreams about their old homeland, and, most importantly, dreams with unpleasant emotions (primarily fear), which we explained by »dream-work«, i.e. some sort of therapeutic »dreaming out« of the experienced trauma;
- Contrary to refugees, non-refugees significantly more often had dreams related to their distant past, dreams related to collective symbols and to group relations.

Having applied statistical confirmation of correlation significance between types, i.e. features of dreams, on one side and certain mental and psychopathological features of subjects on the other, we arrived at the following conclusions:

- Having dreams with trauma is in negative correlation with signs of neuroticism (according to Eysenck) and PTSD -10 Scale symptoms, which led us to confirm, once again, that having dreams with traumatic contents has a positive effect on the stabilisation of the mental state of refugees.

- We determined that dreaming trauma in general and an active attitude in coping with trauma effects are in positive correlation, except for cases of trauma dreaming accompanied by fear (the dreaming of which is in significant negative correlation with an active attitude in coping with trauma effects), which, most probably due to its intensity or personality structure inhibits healthful potentials of the traumatised for coping with trauma effects;
- Dreaming about family has a negative correlation with PTSD symptoms, which indicates a possible protective role of family life in relation to a psychopathological reaction to trauma, except in the cases of depressive dream contents, which in our research positively correlate with family life, the reason of which, we assume, is the loss of important members of immediate family during the long-term refugee life.

Resume

The total sample of 284 subjects – comprising 109 refugees placed at the refugee camp Krnjača (experimental group), and 175 non-refugees (control group), out of which 105 were subjects without any trauma experience whatsoever, and 70 with the experience of somatic trauma – were asked to reply in writing to two questions related to their dreams, as well as to the questions taken from the following instruments: PTSD-10 Scale, Impact of Events Scale, Short Eysenck Personality Inventory and Family Homogeneity Index.

Applying adequate statistical procedures, we tested the significance of differences in the presence of certain features of dreams regarding their formal aspect and the aspect of their contents, i.e. dreaming and dream types (created on the basis of the original classification) between all three subgroups of refugees. The same procedure was applied in determining the significance of correlations between certain psychopathological features of subjects and dream types of refugees.

The research determined that refugees significantly more often described their dreams, as well as that their description was significantly more extensive.

Refugees also had dreams related to their recent past significantly more often, then dreams with trauma contents, especially those coloured by negative emotions and dreams related to war, expulsion, and their old homeland.

Non-refugees, on the other hand, significantly more often had dreams related to their distant past, dreams about human relations and dreams with collective symbols.

Our research determined that fear dreams positively correlate with a passive atti-tude in coping with trauma effects, while dreams about family negatively correlate with PTSD symptoms.

Dreams with trauma contents correlate positively with an active attitude in coping with the effects of refugeeism.

The obtained results were compared to similar studies by other authors.

At the end, we presented a description of dreams in which trauma is evident, as well as those in which refugee trauma becomes recognisable only by performing an interpretation of dreams.

3. Research of Dreams of Somatically Traumatised Subjects

Subjects and instruments

This research of dreams refers to the dreams of 175 subjects. The majority of them, 70 patients, experienced physical trauma. The remaining 105 subjects had no physical trauma in their lives.

The global goal of the quantitative part of this research was to determine the relevance of the correlation between particular dream types and characteristics (dependent on variables) on the one hand, and particular trauma characteristics (somatic, general, with or without co-morbidity, and so on), that is, certain characteristics of psychopathological state of the subjects (general neuroticism or individual neurotic symptoms), on the other.

As to the dependent variables, that is, dream characteristics, we merged two dream classifications. Reference is made to a modern and comprehensive dream classification offered by London Self-Help Line (1999), which divides dreams into 16 types, chiefly by dream content. Those are: collective dreams, death dreams, decision-making dreams, ESP dreams, cure dreams, health-related dreams, sexual dreams, human relations dreams, past-life dreams, lucid dreams, and, finally, nightmares. Kimball's classification (1985), which is older and much narrower (6 dream types), does not overlap with the elements of the former classification generally (which is exactly why we have chosen it) and includes the following dream types: substance-taking dreams, dreams dreamt as a gift, inventive dreams, anticipatory dreams, fear dreams, premonitory dreams, and sadness dreams.

Our dream classification encompasses the elements of both above classifications. We supplemented it with some formal dream features related to the situation itself and the investigation method, such as: extensiveness of dream description, dream commentary, number of described items, time of dreaming, and time in the dream. To those, we added the following characteristics: the general emotional tone of the dream, and the following dream types: group, i.e. family dreams, wishful dreams, dreams about the old homeland, dreams of war, and, finally, dreams related to somatic or physical trauma.

As to the research instruments, they are the same ones mentioned at the very beginning of the book. In this part, we used only the results of the three following instruments: PTSD-10, Brief Personality Inventory according to Eysenck and LEAIQ (Late Effects of Accidental Injury Questionnaire).

From the first two instruments (PTSD-10 and BPI), only total scores from both instruments concerning neuroticism were used, whereas, only variable (item) sets concerning the neurotic characteristics depression, anxiety, insomnia, somatisation, and neurotic cognitive disorders were taken from LEAIQ.

At the very end of the offered instrument set, the subjects were given the two following questions at the top of a blank sheet: »Please describe one or more of your dreams. Please state which period of life they are from.« The subjects were allowed unlimited time for their written answer to those questions and received no oral suggestions during the interview.

Investigation Method

In applying the above mentioned dream classifications and subject characteristics related to trauma, we coded individual written answers about dreams first, relying on the previously done content analysis of described dreams.

Then, statistical data processing was carried out with the aim to establish quantitative values (frequency and percentage) of individual dream characteristics and types in two subject groups - experimental (physically traumatised subjects) and control (experience of mental trauma or without any prior traumatisation). Quantitative values, that is, percentages, of the presence of a particular characteristic were determined in comparison to the total sample (175 subjects), as well as in comparison to the sample of subjects who answered the question about dreams (76 subjects).

Next, the statistical procedure of application of Pearson's χ^2 test for the determination of the statistical significance of differences between the presence of certain dream characteristics in the experimental (physically injured) group and in the control (physically uninjured) was applied.

Finally, statistical significance of correlation between chosen narrower characteristics, that is, types of dreams (dream related to physical trauma, dream related to trauma in general, serial dreams, war in dreams, old homeland in dreams, unpleasant emotions in dreams, fear and depression in a dream and dreams about death), which, from clinical practice, are rightly assumed to be related to some psychopathological state, on the one hand, and certain psychopathological characteristics, on the other. This kind of correlation was tested by linear correlation test. As to the psychopathological characteristics, they refer to overall neuroticism determined on two instruments (PTSD Symptom S% ddcale and Eysenck's Personality Inventory) and some neurotic symptoms from LEAIQ.

Results

Table No. 7 shows the values which are a quantitative expression of responses of all 175 subjects to questions about dreams. It includes subjects without any response to the question whatsoever (returned blank paper) as well as subjects who offered answers such as »I never dream«, »I do not remember my dreams«, and so on. The latter answers are those of subjects who most probably dream but, for reasons unknown to us, claim not to remember their dreams.

Table No. 7: Values of responses to questions about dreams of all subjects

RESPONSES TO QUESTIONS ABOUT DREAMS		SUBJECTS						
1		Somatically traumatised		Somatically non-traumatised		Total		
		f	%	f	%	f	%	
No dream description	Blank page returned	31	17.71	39	22.29	70	40,00	
	I never dream	10	5.71	6	3.43	16	9,14	
	I can never recall my dreams	4	2.29	9	5.14	13	7,43	
	Total	45	25.71	54	30.86	99	56,57	
Dream(s) described		25	14.29	51	29.14	76	43.43	
Total		70	40.00	105	60.00	175	100.00	

Even a cursory glance at Table No. 7 enables an insight into an unexpectedly high number (over half of the subjects - 56.57%) of subjects who refused to describe their dreams. A very high number of subjects who did not answer the question about dreams may be understood chiefly as a result of undeveloped attitude toward the unconscious through dreams in our rationally oriented culture. Or, more specifically, it can be interpreted as an expression of a very present positivistic attitude toward dreams as something confounded, unreasonable, and hence unworthy of attention. The second, perhaps more effective, factor that affected the result is that a part of the subjects was not able to write due to physical injury, which is implied by the fact that the number of sheets returned blank in the experimental group was considerably higher. Finally, it can be a very casual attitude of the pollsters toward subjects, resulting in a missed opportunity to encourage the subjects to answer this last question in the series without influencing the content of responses to questions about dreams. But such a result in terms of dreams of the injured is not unusual. Thus, Schenck and Mahowald (1991) found that sleeping disorders or unpleasant dreams remained entirely undiagnosed until the introduction of polysomnography in out-patients and those admitted for surgical procedures. Their finding was that as many as 15% of those who claimed not to dream actually suffered from nightmares.

We also confirmed the findings mentioned in literature (Kimball 1985) that about 5% (more precisely, from 3.43% in the control group to 9.14% in the total sample) of people claim that they never dream. The percentage of those who do dream but regularly forget their dreams or do not have a habit of remembering them is somewhat lower (2.29-7.43%). In interviews with people who claimed to do so, in the psychotherapeutic situation, we noticed that those are usually fragments of scenes, without emotional tones, which are forgotten soon after waking up unless they are paid special attention to.

Table No. 8 presents numerical values (frequencies and respective percentages) of a series of dream characteristics and types, encompassing responses of all 175 subjects, that is, answers of 76 subjects who described their dreams, respectively.

The table indicates that the subjects, when describing their dreams, most often (in about 50% of the cases) did it in a moderately extensive manner, i.e. in 8-10 sentences. However, this was significantly more frequent in the control, i.e. the group without physical trauma (χ^2=5.18; p=0.0228; df=1). The remaining quarter of cases described their dreams either in a mere sentence or two, or at length - half a page to one entire page.

Dreams were commented on by less than 10% of all subjects, that is, only 15% (each seventh subject) of those who presented their dreams. This also corresponds to the educational structure of the subjects, since dreams were interpreted by either highly educated subjects or those who are less educated but firmly rooted in tradition, and who interpreted their dreams according to folk beliefs. There were statistically significantly more commentaries in the group of somatically traumatised subjects, which may lead to the assumption that the need of the physically injured to understand or explain their dreams was stronger than in the control. This assumption is, however, annulled by the result that the controls (see Table No. 9) had significantly more dreams which were more lengthily described, that is, more subjects who offered more than one dream. Healthier subjects in the control group were, nevertheless, significantly more willing to participate in the part of the research that dealt with their dreams.

Over 50% of the described dreams were dreamt in the present and the same percentage of their content also concerned the present. As high a percentage (20-40%) of the described dreams concerned the immediate past. This was especially apparent in the group with somatic traumas, whereas the percentage of dreams dreamt during childhood or with childhood content was nearly 20% in the control, in contrast to 80% of childhood dreams in the experimental group. It should be added, however, that the differences were not confirmed statistically. Namely, this result does not completely affirm the assumption that physical trauma had a stronger impact on the visual content of dreaming. It is very probable that trauma has a stronger impact on the occurrence of emotions in dreams; and their specific weight in interpretation of dreams is bigger than that of dream images or scenes anyway (Opalić 1999).

Table No. 8. Values (frequency and percentages) of particular dream characteristics and types in the subjects' answers

| DREAM CHARACTERISTICS | | SUBJECTS | | | | | | | | |
Broader	Narrower	f	A-% (70)	B-% (25)	f	A-% (105)	B-% (51)	f	A-% (175)	B-% (76)
			Somatically traumatised			Somatically non-traumatised			Total	
Extensiveness of dream description	Short	9	12.86	36.00	13	12.38	25.49	22	12.57	28.95
	Moderately extensive	10	14.29	40.00	32	30.48	62.75	42	24.00	55.26
	Very extensive	6	8.57	24.00	6	5.71	11.76	12	6.86	15.79
With commentary about the dream		7	10.00	28.00	5	4.76	9.80	12	6.86	15.79
Number of described dreams	One	14	20.00	56.00	32	30.48	62.75	46	26.29	60.53
	Two	5	7.14	20.00	3	2.86	5.88	8	4.57	10.53
	Three or more	4	5.71	16.00	16	15.24	31.37	20	11.43	26.32
When did you dream the mentioned dream	*childhood	2	2.86	8.00	10	9.52	19.61	12	6.86	15.79
	*immediate past	8	11.43	32.00	17	16.19	33.33	25	14.29	32.89
	Present	15	21.43	60.00	27	25.71	52.94	42	24.00	55.26
To which period of your life did the dream refer to	*childhood	2	2.86	8.00	11	10.48	21.57	13	7.43	17.11
	*immediate past	10	14.29	40.00	11	10.48	21.57	21	12.00	27.63
	Present	12	17.14	48.00	30	28.57	58.82	42	24.00	55.26
Emotionality of dreams	No emotions	1	1.43	4.00	1	0.95	1.96	2	1.14	2.63
	Pleasant emotions	9	12.86	36.00	21	20.00	41.18	30	17.14	39.47
	Unpleasant emotions	8	11.43	32.00	28	26.67	54.90	36	20.57	47.37
	unpleasant emotion → woke you up	8	11.43	32.00	9	8.57	17.65	17	9.71	22.37
	Fear in dream	13	18.57	52.00	19	18.10	37.25	32	30.48	42.11
	Depression in dream	4	5.71	16.00	14	13.33	27.45	18	10.29	23.68
Dream types	Psychotic in a narrow sense	1	1.43	4.00	2	1.90	3.92	3	1.71	3.95
	Group dream in general	10	14.29	40.00	12	11.43	23.53	22	12.57	28.95
	Group dream about family	6	8.57	24.00	13	12.38	25.49	19	10.86	25.00
	About war	9	12.86	36.00	8	7.62	15.69	17	9.71	22.37
	Wishful dream	10	14.29	40.00	25	23.81	49.02	35	20.00	46.05
	About old homeland	7	10.00	28.00	6	5.71	11.76	13	7.43	17.11
	*Dream recurrence (serial dreams)	8	11.43	32.00	23	21.90	45.10	31	17.71	40.79
	*About trauma in general	8	11.43	32.00	15	14.29	29.41	23	13.14	30.26
	*About physical trauma	10	14.29	40.00	2	1.90	3.92	12	6.85	15.79
	*Prophetic dream	3	4.29	12.00	6	5.71	11.76	9	5.14	11.84
	*Collective dream	1	1.43	4.00	13	12.38	25.49	14	8.00	18.42
	*Decision-making dream	1	1.43	4.00	0	0	0	1	0.57	1.32
	*Healing-hinting dream	3	4.29	12.00	5	4.76	9.80	8	4.57	10.53
	*About relations with other people	9	12.86	36.00	32	30.48	62.75	41	23.43	53.95
	*With sexual contents	0	0	0	5	4.76	9.80	5	2.86	6.580
	*About death	3	4.29	12.00	11	10.48	21.57	14	8.00	18.42
	*With ESP	0	0	0	0	0	0	0	0	0
	*About health problems	5	7.14	20.00	3	2.86	5.88	8	4.57	10.53

*   Dream characteristics and types according to Self-Help Line (1999) and Kimball (1985)
**   A-%= percentage of the dream characteristic or type in the total sample
*** B-%= percentage of the dream characteristic or type in the sample of subjects who answered the questions about dreams

40% of the subjects in the experimental group, i.e. subjects with physical injury experience, indeed dreamt about trauma-related contents. This approximates the percentage (47%) of the subjects, war veterans, who reported dreaming details from fighting in similar researches (Esposito et al. 1999).

Table No. 9 shows only the dream characteristics whose significant presence was statistically confirmed, either in the experimental group of somatically traumatised individuals in comparison to the same characteristics in the control group of somatically non-traumatised, or vice versa.

The key result we obtained in this research is the one concerned with statistically more significantly present dream contents related to physical trauma in the experimental group, who had been traumatised in reality, in both calculation methods (first for all subjects: (χ^2=13.82; p=0.0002). In other words, physical injury is also a psychological trauma *par excellence* which leaves its imprint on dream content as well.

Moreover, physically injured subjects usually dream about details, that is, about the situation which led to their injury as a rule. This conclusion has been substantial, with the following two results showing that in the experimental group, there were significantly more war-related dream contents (χ^2=3.99; p=0.0459) and significantly more (although at the level of statistical trend: χ^2=3.55; p=0.0595) dream contents related to physical injury, most probably those related to the current physical injury (Table No. 9).

In psychoanalytic terminology, dreaming of a trauma-related content is the work of dream, a processing of trauma - and a very successful one at that, since better adapted persons dream about trauma they have experienced more often than less adapted ones (Peretz, Kaminer 1991). We should recall that some dream researchers (Hartman 1991) assume that there are, in principle, two possible types of trauma-related dreams. Dreams of the first kind improve the contact with the traumatic event, whereas the dreams of the second, less desirable, type prevent the replaying of trauma. Our research confirms the prevalence of the first type of dream.

Further, our research determined that there were significantly more unpleasant emotions (by both calculation methods) in the group of subjects who did not experience physical trauma (Table No. 9). This result is in concordance with the following one, where more repetitive dreams occurred in the group without traumatic experience (though at the level of the statistical trend: χ^2=3.37; p=0.0662). Thus, in the control group, there were significantly more unpleasant emotions »processed« in serial dreams and most probably related to coping with unpleasant feelings caused by trauma. This conclusion is supported by the result (Table No. 10) that unpleasant emotions have a negative correlation with the overall neuroticism of the subjects (according to Eysenck) as well as with the fear of trauma-like situations, which is one of the PTSD symptoms. Research by Stepansky and collaborators (1988) in which out of 1,000 randomly chosen subjects from Australia, only 55 had emotionally coloured dreams (10% dreams with negative, 20% positive and 29% neutral emotions) supports the conclusion that a very high percentage of subjects with negative emotions in dreams in our research (40%) probably results from the stressful situation in which the entire Serbian population has been living for the last decade (10% of the population are refugees; total external blockade introduced against Yugoslavia, multiple drop of the standard of living in comparison to previous years, etc.).

Table No. 9: Values of parameters of statistically significant differences between the presence of specific dream characteristics in the somatically traumatised (experimental) group and somatically non-traumatised (control) group of subjects

NARROWER DREAM CHARACTERISTIC (GROUP IN WHICH THE CHARACTERISTIC IS STATISTICALLY MORE SIGNIFICANTLY PRESENT)	VALUES OF PARAMETERS OF STATISTICALLY SIGNIFICANT DIFFERENCES BETWEEN THE EXPERIMENTAL GROUP (70) AND THE CONTROLS (105) IN THE TOTAL SAMPLE (175)			VALUES OF PARAMETERS OF STATISTICALLY SIGNIFICANT DIFFERENCES BETWEEN THE EXPERIMENTAL GROUP (25) AND THE CONTROLS (51) IN THE SAMPLE SUBJECTS WHO DESCRIBED THEIR DREAMS (76)		
1	χ^2	p	Degrees of freedom	χ^2	p	Degrees of freedom
Contents related to physical trauma (more in the experimental)	8.23	0.0041	1	13.82	0.0002	1
Negative emotionality (more in the control)	5.07	0.0243	1	3.53	0.0603 (trend)	1
War in dreams (more in the experimental)				3.99	0.0459	1
Dream recurrence (more in the control)	3.37	0.0662 (trend)	1			
Health problems (more in the experimental)				3.55	0.0595 (trend)	1
Collective symbols in dreams (more in the control)	6.88	0.0087	1	5.08	0.0242	1
Relationships with other people (more in the control)	9.73	0.0018	1	7.91	0.0047	1
Moderately extensive description (more in the control)	5.18	0.0228	1	3.51	0.0610 (trend)	1
With dream commentary (more in the experimental)				4.18	0.0410	1
Two described dreams (more in the experimental)				3.55	0.0595 (trend)	1

Very probably, it was because of dreaming physical injuries as such that a release of negative emotions related to them occurred. But, as it seems, traumatism of physical injuries is permanently marked by the injury situation, i.e., war, which was dreamt more often in the experimental, physically injured, group - as determined in our previous researches.

This research shows that physically traumatised dreamers tend less to dream dreams which are assessed as complex in the qualitative sense. Those are dreams with collective symbols, which were significantly more frequent in the subject group without physical trauma (also confirmed by the total dreamers' sample).

In the control group, there were also significantly more dreams concerning relationships with other people. It is difficult to explain which factor had the strongest impact on this result. Additional research (whose results have not been presented in the tabular form), however, indicate that some socio-demographic characteristics of the subjects may also be involved. Namely, subjects aged under 50 dreamt dreams with negative emotions significantly more frequently (χ^2=11.52; p=0.0092; df=3). Such dreams were significantly more frequently dreamt by women (χ^2=5.64; p=0.0175; df=1), then, more frequently by single subjects than married ones (χ^2=4.01; p=0.0451; df=1), more frequently by blue-collar workers, students and soldiers than white-collar workers and pensioners (χ^2=19.32; p=0.0132; df=8). Moreover, women dreamt about death significantly more frequently (χ^2=1.13; p=0.0422; df=1). Hopf's research (1992) also shows that women, i.e., girls dream emotionally coloured dreams (especially those involving aggression) significantly more frequently. If we consider the fact that there were more women, either single or married, in the control group (in absolute numbers, first of all), then the above mentioned demographic characteristics have played a certain role in the findings that there were significantly more negative emotions in the dreams of subjects without any physical trauma.

The results of statistical comparison of certain psychopathological characteristics of the subjects on the one hand, and of dream characteristics that are traumatogenic in one way or another on the other, obtained by calculation of linear correlations between the variables, are shown in Table No. 10.

Table No. 10: Statistically significant correlations between characteristics of trauma-related dreams and the psychological status of the subject
[somatically traumatised=E(70); C=somatically non-traumatised (105), total sample=E+C /175)]

DREAM CHARACTE-RISTICS	PSYCHOPATHOLOGICAL STATUS OF THE SUBJECT										
	Total value on the PTSD-10 scale		Neuroticism (acc. to Eysenck)		One of the PTSD symptoms (PTSD scale)		One of the overall neurotic symptoms from LEAIQ		Derangement symptom	
	E	E+C	E	E+C	E	E+C	E	E+C	E	E+C
Physical trauma-related dream					Choking r = 0.27; p = 0.011 Fear of trauma-like situations r = -0.25; p = 0.018		Depression r = 0.30; p = 0.006 Cognitive inhibition r = 0.28; p = 0.009	Somatisation r = 0.15; p = 0.025		
War in dream	r = -0.23 p = 0.030	r = -0.17 p = 0.012	r = -0.29 p = 0.010		Nightmare r = -0.26 p = 0.014	Nightmare r = -0.20 p = 0.003	Somatisation r = 0.20; p = 0.000 Insomnia r = 0.13; p = 0.047			r = -0.21 p = 0.003
Old homeland in dream	r = -0.25 p = 0.018	r = -0.17 p = 0.012	r = -0.21 p = 0.048	r = -0.15 p = 0.027	Nightmare r = -0.24 p = 0.023	Fear of trauma-like situations r = -0.28 p = 0.000	Somatisation r = 0.20; p = 0.045 Insomnia r = 0.32; p = 0.003	Depression r = 0.18; p = 0.007 Somatisation r = 0.19; p = 0.005 Insomnia r = 0.26; p = 0.000 Anxiety r = 0.16; p = 0.017		r = -0.16 p = 0.016
Negative emotionality in dream			r = -0.15 p = 0.026		Thoughts about trauma r = 0.23; p = 0.039 Fear of trauma-like situations r = -0.24; p = 0.022		Insomnia r = 0.13; p = 0.029			
Dream series, that is, dream repetition	r = -0.25 p = 0.017		r = -0.14 p = 0.035		Thoughts about trauma r = 0.22; p = 0.040 Fear of trauma-like situations r = 0.13; p = 0.049	Nightmare r = 0.13; p = 0.098	Somatisation r = 0.24; p = 0.021 Insomnia r = 0.26; p = 0.016	Anxiety r = 0.27; p = 0.000	r = -0.26 p = 0.014	

The dream characteristic designated as physical trauma dreaming does not correlate positively with any summary result of neuroticism (either according to Eysenck or with the total score from the PTSD scale). That is to say that physical injury of the subjects leaves visible traces in dreams only in positive correlation with individual neurotic symptoms, with the feeling of choking ($r=0.27$; $p=0.011$), depression ($r=0.30$; $p=0.006$), cognitive inhibition ($r=0.28$; $p=0.009$), and somatisation ($r=0.019$; $p=0.025$). Actually, it is in negative correlation with fear of trauma-like situations from the PTSD scale ($r=0.25$; $p=0.018$).

Our results indicate that general trauma (very probably from one's earlier past) is chiefly processed down to its traces in dreams, since its dreaming is in no correlation with any general or specific neurotic symptoms of the subjects.

However, characteristics of dreams about wars or the old homeland do correlate with certain elements of the psychopathological status of the subjects. It is interesting that the correlations are between those characteristics and overall neurotic symptoms (dreams about war in three calculation methods, and dreams about old homeland in as many as four calculation methods). This supports the conclusion that dreaming about earlier traumatogenic events related to war or loss of homeland (for refugees especially) has been effective in terms of stabilisation of the psychological state. To be more specific, dreaming dreams with such content helped in the re-constellation of threat as the chief negative emotion in trauma. It also decreased general neurotic effects of trauma, which, nevertheless, was not wiped completely from the (unconscious) memory. This is supported by positive correlations between dreaming about war, especially about the old homeland, and individual neurotic symptoms (obtained from several items in Late Effects of Accident Questionnaire) belonging to the developed neurotic clinical picture. Those are insomnia and somatisation (for correlations with dreams about war and the old homeland) as well as depression and anxiety (for correlations with dreams about the old homeland).

On the other hand, correlations of dreams about war and old homeland with certain PTSD symptoms are negative (especially with nightmares and fear of trauma-like situations) (Table No. 10). This is suggestive of the assumption that those dream contents have a positive effect on the disappearance of PTSD symptoms, which was also confirmed in the practice of offering psychotherapeutic help to refugees, i.e., the wounded.

The same conclusion is true for the neurotic symptom of »derangement«, which we previously found to be the most specific neurotic symptom of our subjects. Since it is in negative correlation with dreaming about war and the old homeland, it can be classified into specific PTSD symptoms of our subjects.

The assumption that the repetition of a dream (or serial dreams) is an indication of so-called dream work, i.e., function of »emotional detoxification« which dreams have in removing traumatisation effects, has been proved to be mostly true in our research.

In other words, repetition of dreams, in our research, is in negative correlation with both the total value on the PTSD scale and neuroticism according to Eysenck's Personality Inventory. However, repetition of dream does not yet fully achieve its positive effect in alleviating negative emotions of the injured, that is, in redefining his/her existence in new life circumstances. Dream repetition correlates positively with as many as three PTSD symptoms (thoughts about trauma, fear of trauma-like situations, and nightmares) as well as with three neurotic symptoms from the LAEQ (somatisation, anxiety, and insomnia) (Table No. 10).

Qualitative Overview of Subjects' Dreams

The above quantitative analysis offered a partial insight into some patterns of relations between certain dream characteristics on the one hand, and the psychological state of physically traumatised subjects on the other. But, in view of the imaginatively oneiric and - in some well grounded opinions (Hobson 1998) - even hallucinatory, that is, delirious character of dreams, it has been and remains abstract. Hence, for the purpose of authenticity of the entire research and for the illustration of the above analysis, we shall present certain dreams in their original narrative, i.e., phenomenal form, in the words of our subjects, as given when describing their dreams. The subjects with somatic trauma answered the two questions about dreams chiefly in hospital, during their treatment, whereas their controls answered the questions at their homes or at work. Instead of an extensive description of the overall social climate in which the dreams were dreamt (a year before the NATO bombing of Yugoslavia), we would like to draw your attention to the fact that this was a time of general pauperisation of the Serbian population, of an increase in the number of psychiatric disorders of responsive character, and of a drastic drop in the standard of living and almost all indicators of the population health status. That was the time of conflicts in the political scene, mass protests in Serbia, and the exodus of Serbs from other parts of former Yugoslavia to Serbia and Montenegro, where some 800,000 refugees found a safe haven.

The dreams presented are accompanied by a brief commentary and basic biographic details about their respective dreamers. A deeper interpretation of dreams would require a presentation of the theoretical framework of their interpretation, which is in essence existential-analytical (Opalić 1988, 1999, 2000). In our opinion, that would reduce the authenticity and polysemy of associations usually produced by emotionally rich contents found in the material offered by dream contents.

Due to the basic character of the research, the dreams are divided into two groups: dreams of somatically non-traumatised subjects and dreams of physically injured subjects.

a) Dreams of somatically non-traumatised subjects

For some subjects, judging by the content of the dreams they recall, earlier traumas occurred mostly within the family. This is true for the dream of a 34-year-old pre-school teacher, a mother of two children, who recalls a dream dreamt ten years ago.

Dream: *I dreamt about my sister's son, who was a boy then, actually a small child. In the dream, I took his arm, which I had found torn off in a park. I have been and still am very attached to him. I love him very much. Perhaps because he was the first male child in our family for a long time. That scene from my dream with his torn-off arm often appears in my dreams, which I usually cannot recall.*

Similar in its character to this one (processing of earlier traumatic events related to personal development, that is, the loss of the loved ones, and very probably provoked by the current difficult social situation) is the dream of a 27-year old unemployed high-school graduate living with her father, mother and brother in Belgrade.

Dream: *I have been dreaming this dream for a long time - for the last five to six years. My tragically deceased aunt, to whom many of my pleasant memories are re-lated, is in the dream. We talk in the dream. She is seriously ill, we are parting. We both know that the end is imminent, that it can happen any moment. I cry, sob and wake crying.*

The following dreams were dreamt by a 47-year-old lady, an employed pedagogy teacher living in Belgrade with her husband and adopted 7-year old son, who is fairly well-off. They own two business premises with a large bookshop. Lately, she has been dreaming two types of dreams occurring in a series.

1st dream type: *I buy some beautiful things in wonderful shops abroad. Everything is in beautiful colours. I wake up joyful.*

2nd dream type: *I dream that my child has fallen into muddy water and I cannot see him or get him out. I wake up afraid and in a bad mood.*

It is interesting that, among other subjects, there were also those whose traumatic dream contents are related to the World War II when Belgrade was bombed twice, by Nazi Germany in 1941 and by the Allies in 1944. Thus, a 60-year-old Belgrade lady describes her childhood dreams which, obviously due to their traumatism, are deeply etched in her memory.

Dream: *From my childhood, I remember my dreams about war, bombing, trenches, and tanks, which were then very frequent and very unpleasant. From my later years, I recall only dreams about flying.*

The following are three dreams of a 23-year-old young man, an information sci-ence student living with his mother and grandmother in a small town near Belgrade. They are illustrative since they are from three different periods of his life, reflecting the current existential problems which he has been encountering in his environment.

69

The last of the three indirectly expresses a difficult social climate in which the Serbian population lives.

1st dream (from his early childhood): *I walk down a street. I see a pool with some shoes in it. I step onto the shoes and at that moment start falling down through a deep abyss. Still falling, I wake up frightened.*

2nd dream (approximately at the age of 15): *I walk the streets of the neighbourhood I live in. Suddenly, I start flying. I consider this normal, I even feel nice. Thus flying, I greet my friends, fly through houses, rooms, under a bridge... I used to dream this same dream for years.*

3rd dream (at the time of research): *There has been a big catastrophe. I learn that the Moon has fallen down onto the planet Earth. I smell sulphur and smoke. Around me, there is a multitude of people who are all somehow bewildered. There are also many casualties. The whole time, I am running through the town streets and watching the horrible scenes, until I wake up upset.*

The dream of a 33-year-old mechanical engineer, who lives with his wife and two daughters in Belgrade, may be considered typical of processing the experience of the difficult times and social circumstances at the time it was dreamt.

Dream: *There are many soldiers around. World War I is in progress. There are many dead in the pits and around them. The pits are covered with planks, and the soldiers who survived cross along the planks or between the pits. The soldiers are in the Serbian uniforms. It is interesting that there are no wounded. Everything is full of smoke, fog and soot. It is cold. There is no sound from anywhere. Everything is soundless. Then I wake up.*

The following are dreams of a 49-year-old clerk who comes from the former Republic Srpska Krajina, now Republic of Croatia. With his wife and two children, the dreamer has been living in Belgrade for 20 years already.

Dream series: *Lately and relatively frequently, I have been dreaming about my hometown, which is today practically deserted. The entire Serb population has been evicted from their homes. While the military operations lasted there, I dreamt that I was with them, too. Afterwards, after the combat activities stopped, I dream about going to the homeland, with all the details of places, landscapes, even colours, but with unpleasant feelings with which I finally wake up.*

Dreams of a 57-year-old pensioner from Belgrade, a father of two daughters, are of similar character.

Dream series: *I dream about my birthplace, which is now in another country, Croatia, »Uncle Franjo's«... I also dream about the hospital and doctors at the Intensive care Unit... I dream about water, i.e. the canal into which I once jumped and had a heart attack... I dream about medications, which I cannot find on prescription in state-owned pharmacies and have no money to buy in privately-owned ones.*

Subsequently, here are the dreams which, were it not for the difficult circumstances in our country, could be rightly classified as predictive, anticipatory dreams, since they are from the time of several years before the NATO bombing of Yugoslavia related to the conflicts in Kosovo. The first was dreamt by a 23-year-old young man and the second by a 34-year-old man from Belgrade.

1st dream: *One afternoon, I am returning home from downtown, and when I am passing by the place where I often used to play as a child, war planes start flying over and go on to bomb the neighbourhood in which I used to live. A plane flies over, just overhead, so that I have to lie down beside a concrete pillar by which I often used to play as a child. I cannot recall anything else.*

2nd dream: *I dream about the bombing of military targets in the vicinity of Belgrade. The rest of the city is peaceful. That is all.*

It is an open question whether the dream of a 22-year-old young lady, a Belgrade clerk, who dreams that her teeth have fallen out, can be classified into the same category. Or, whether this is simply a dream expressing fear coloured with depression. It is Serbian folk belief (Čajkanović 1970) that dreams about losing teeth (or a tooth) are an omen of imminent death in the family.

Dream: *I have dreamt repeatedly that I had been left without any teeth in my dream. I stand in front of a mirror and cannot believe that my teeth are falling out, one by one. My hand is full of teeth. I am thinking how I am to go out so toothless. And amid the chaos, derangement, nervousness and grief, I wake up.*

b) Dreams of somatically traumatised subjects at war and in peacetime

First, we present a dream of a 24-year-old locksmith, a fighter from the Bosnian war, characteristic of the period immediately after his leg was wounded. It illustrates the detoxifying but nightmarish character of such dreams.

I dreamt this dream the first night after the wounding. We work in a terrain. Our task is to free some guys who are surrounded. There is some kind of fog and the road ahead of us can barely be seen. And there is some ditch with muddy water. We are to set off. Then a truck with soldiers comes. They are Muslims. I take the rocket launcher, shoot at the truck and miss. They discover us, jump out of the truck and shoot at us. Next to me, there is my commander who is shot in the belly and is trying to hold his intestines in. he falls into the water ditch, and it is not water but blood and in it there is my friend - headless. One can hear scrams, cries for help, moaning, and shots. Then, I hear shells fired from their side. I shout: »Watch it, mortars!« At that moment, something red appears in front of me. I feel the detonation and pain in my chest, arms, and legs. I think: »Here I die«, moan and wake up in a hospital bed all sweated up and frightened. A nurse entered the room then and asked me: »What is the matter?« I

71

told her: »I had a bad dream.« I took a cigarette and smoked, praying that my friends had not got killed.

Here is a dream of an 18-year-old Belgrade girl who injured her leg in an auto accident.

The dream is from the period of my life after the accident, immediately, i.e., a day after the accident. The face of the young man who drove the car and hit me appears before my eyes and mocks me ironically. He is telling me something about the event, he is rude, ironic. After that dream I saw the face of the sordid bum in every man.

Prophetic dreams were also dreamt by persons wounded in the battlefields. This happened to a 23-year-old farmer, who fought in the Republic Srpska, Republic Bosnia and Herzegovina, wounded in the leg. He reports:

Dream: *When I was at the frontline, I dreamt a dream which remains etched in my memory. I dreamt about having been wounded in my left leg. And only a couple of days later, that was just what really happened. That I dream and can so predict what will happen, I have found hard to understand to this day.*

We shall describe a dream and the specific dissociative phenomenon accompanying it which we (Opalić 1999, p. 195) have noticed earlier, terming it *déjà vu* (already dreamt). In this phenomenon, a dreamer feels that what (s)he experiences in reality (situation people, and so on) constitutes details or a major part of her/his recent dream. The dream we report was dreamt by a 35-year-old shop assistant living with her daughter, son and husband in Belgrade. She dreamt it after a surgery of her ankle, which was injured at her job. It should be mentioned that her parents fled from the Republic Srpska Krajina and live in a collective refugee accommodation centre near Belgrade.

Dream: *A few days before I broke my ankle, I dreamt that I was with my parents, who are accommodated in the Despotovac centre. A kolo was being danced there. The music was playing. I wanted to join the kolo and to start dancing, but my mother would not let me. She was pushing me away from the dancers. And they, the dancers and musicians, looked like horned devils, black and hairy. After she had pushed me, my mother, together with my sister-in-law (deceased five years before), went to some cellar and I went with them. And there, there were many children and grown-ups. Somehow, I managed to get out of there, while my mother and sister-in-law remained there.*

The *déjà vu* (already dreamt) phenomenon in the original version of the subject was reported like this:

When I fell and broke my leg I cried: »Oh, mother, mother!« My neighbours, husband and son came to help and drove me to the hospital in an ambulance. As soon as I entered the hall of the Emergency Centre, and the hall was dark, I recalled my dream. That was the one, the same dark room, the cellar from my dream. Next to me, a 10-year-old boy was brought, all in blood. There were many people with serious injuries, many children and elderly. The boy was crying that he was going to die. His bewildered parents came in. I cried and forgot about my ankle. There, that is how I remember both the break and the dream dreamt before I even broke my leg and the peculiar coincidence between the dream and the experienced.

The following dream is typical, one would say, of refugees. This impression was gained based on interviews with many refugees, including their relatives. It was dreamt by a 34-year-old soldier from the Bosnian war, with a thigh wound that later got infected.

Dream: *I am walking the streets of a familiar town. The town used to be busy, full of beauty and freshness. However, that day, the town is completely different. The streets are deserted, not a living soul can be seen. The war is raging. The enemy hit from everywhere, but the people are resisting, they are not surrendering. Far away, cannon fire can be heard and the air I breathe is full of gunpowder and I can feel some danger in the air. The buildings are tall and look somehow spooky in the silence. In my dream, I fall asleep and look at myself. I am in my combat uniform, slightly worn and stained with blood in some places. In my hand, I hold a machine gun from which cartridge belts hang down dragging along the road. I look around then and stop. I see a fire start, engulfing everything before it. It spreads and gets closer and closer to me. The town is aflame and simply vanishing before my eyes. With it, I am vanishing, too, standing there and looking into the distance.*

Even more striking are the dreams whose content constitutes processing of traumatic events experienced by fighters at the frontline. The dreamer of the following one was injured in the Bosnian war and treated, just like the previous subject, for multiple wounds at the Orthopaedic Hospital of the University Clinical Centre, Belgrade. Here is how he describes his dreams and comments on them:

1ˢᵗ dream: *Twenty days after the wounding, I dreamt about my hometown and the town where I lived, Mrkonjić Grad. It had fallen under the occupation of the Croat armed forces, which distressed me more than my wounding did. The thoughts about the events going on there suppressed almost any worry about myself and my wounding. According to the Dayton treaty, Mrkonjić grad was to be returned to the Serbs, but the Croats were burning it down systematically, so as to return as little as possible to us. That December night, I dreamt that I was watching my street. It was all sunlit. I saw my house and my granny's house clearly. They were entirely whole and undamaged. As if something was telling me: »It's all right, you are still lucky!« With this pleasant feeling, I woke up and the entire next day went nicely. That day, we even got the news that our houses had not been touched. The news came from our friends, Croats, who remained in the town.*

2ⁿᵈ dream: *Recently, I dreamt a dream again in which I am in front of the gate to our house. Naturally, I wish to go in at once, but I do not head for the front door. Something tells me to go in through a side room which I had turned into a workshop, to see whether my tools have been taken. The door is closed and it seems as if nothing has been taken. When I push the door, however, I feel an explosion, which startles me but I do not wake up. A thought crosses my mind: »The door was booby-trapped but I am not hurt, even the door is not damaged.« But when I go in, the room is all scorched and empty. With an unpleasant feeling that everything I have has been taken away and destroyed, I woke up.*

Are my covert fears justified? Will I ever be able to return home?

Here is how a 40-year-old worker, a father of two children, who fought in the Bosnian war, describes and comments his dreams.

1st dream: *After being wounded, I had quite disturbing dreams. In one of them, I am at Gradačac frontline. We were going to take a nearby village. There were awfully large numbers of dead, wounded and massacred. That distressed me so much that I gave a start in my sleep, and almost fell off the bed. I was simultaneously frightened and happy about it being only a dream.*

2nd dream: *I remember a dream I dreamt at the time immediately after being wounded, in Brčko hospital. I dreamt that I was killed. I dreamt all sorts of things as in the previous dream. I got scared, jerked and woke up. For a moment, I was happy because it was not real, but I could not fall asleep again after the terrible dream.*

A 26-year-old young man, who has lost both legs in the Bosnian war, dreams wishful dreams (that he has legs, etc.). In those terms, he proceeds with his thoughts about himself, his destiny, giving his conclusion, in a resigned and deeply humane manner, about the senselessness of war and the ephemeral role of an individual in it. Here are his words:

This is from the period of my »second life«. I dreamt that I had legs, that I walked, had a job and decent life, and that I would not go to war any more and would not have to take a gun in my hands for other people's ideas any more. I dreamt that I had a family and children and that I played with them as did their mother. For I am incapable of doing any of it now.

Finally, in a kind of conclusion to the presented dreams, we will report a dream of a 28-year-old Belgrade carpenter, a father of one child, born in Belgrade. In an almost collectively symbolic manner, the dream expresses the sum and substance of a situation of a person threatened by actual and potential traumatisation.

Dream: *Slowly, walking along railway rails, I skip over to every second sleeper. A train is approaching at high speed, but I am not afraid of it. I carry a bird in a cage. The bird is small, yellow and frightened. I tell it that everything is all right and that we are in no danger. The bird does not understand me and I am sad because of that.*

Is the bird in this dream a representative of the individual human courage and unalienable freedom of an individual to persevere despite danger threatening him on his way? Or is the bird, if the dream is understood as an expression of collective symbolism, a figure whom the dreamer has set apart to be afraid on the railroad of historical existence instead of him, i.e., his people? What the man will do, or, what we will do, faced with the iron dragon charging at us, was not dreamt by our subject. Are we, either individually or collectively as a nation, to »dream out« or, better put, to redefine in reality what is real and what is an oneiric danger to us individually or collectively? It remains to be seen. Anyway, dreaming, we increase the probability of finding the right solution for a free and relaxed existence of us all, individually and collectively.

Conclusions

On the sample of 175 subjects, 76 of which answered the question about dreams, the first finding was that a very large number of subjects (over one-half) refused to answer the question about dreams. Of the 76 subjects who did answer it, as many as 30% claimed that they either never dreamt, or that they dream but cannot recall their dreams. Similar findings were also obtained by other researchers of dreams of the physically injured, since the number of subjects who did not describe their dreams in our research was considerably higher in the somatically traumatised (experimental) group. Subjects either with general trauma or without any traumatic experience described their dreams in a manner that was statistically significantly lengthier; the frequency of their reporting two or more dreams was statistically significantly higher.

In employing an extensive classification of dream characteristics and types, we found that physical trauma-related dream contents are processed in the dreams of physically traumatised individuals significantly more frequently than in the controls. Moreover, in the physically injured group, there were significantly more dreams about war as well as dream contents related to health problems.

Our conclusion is that dreaming about trauma, in the experimental group, is a type of individual processing of trauma, a kind of mental detoxification. That this is indeed a process of coping with trauma effects in dreams about trauma itself is confirmed by a positive correlation between dreaming about physical trauma and only a few neurotic symptoms (depression, neurotic cognitive inhibition, and somatisation) and some PTSD symptoms (choking and fear of trauma-like situations).

In the experimental group, there were significantly more dreams related to war and the old homeland; and those characteristics correlate negatively with the overall neuroticism of the subjects examined by means of Eysenck's Inventory and the PTSD scale, which supports the view of positive therapeutic effects in dreaming such dreams. However, dreaming about physical trauma also correlates positively with several individual symptoms of neurosis, i.e., PTSD, which means that physical trauma remains present in the subjective life of the injured.

It is interesting that we found that there were significantly more negative emotions and recurrent dreams in the group of physically uninjured individuals, that is, in the subgroups of female and single subjects. Since there were as many as 40% of subjects who dreamt dreams with negative emotionality in our sample, it may be assumed that this result was affected by overall social circumstances in our country, which is also implied by the results of some other researchers.

The physically traumatised dream fewer so-called complex dreams, i.e., dreams with collective symbols concerning relationships with other people.

As to overall traumatism, it correlates with no neurotic symptom whatsoever. It may be that trauma remains in memory as a conscious cognitive, that is, perceptive, trace, rationally integrated into the psychological life of an individual.

Since the correlations between war and the old homeland in dreams on the one hand and individual PTSD symptoms (fear of trauma-like situations, nightmares, including the most frequent phenomenon of »derangement«) on the other are negative, it may be concluded that dreaming traumatic events has a therapeutic (detoxifying) effect, primarily in elimination of some PTSD symptoms.

In our research, dream recurrence was confirmed to be an effective method of processing negative trauma effects, since we found negative correlation between dream series, on the one hand, and overall neuroticism of the subjects (both on Eysenck's Inventory and PTSD scale), on the other. This detoxifying function of serial dreams is not final, since repetitive dreams are in a positive correlation with certain subjects' psychopathological characteristics, which belong to the array of PTSD (thoughts about trauma and fear of trauma-like situations), as well as with some general neurotic symptoms (anxiety and insomnia).

A good portion of the results of the previous quantitative analysis is vividly illustrated with examples of concrete dreams of all subjects, dreams dominated by war scenes and negative emotionality.

Resume

The sample of 70 patients hospitalised due to severe somatic injuries (26 injured at war and 44 in peacetime) who were in the experimental group, and 105 subjects without any somatic injury (45 of them with no trauma experience whatsoever) in the healthy controls, were tested by the following instruments: Impact of Events Scale, PTSD-10 Scale, Brief Eysenck's Personality Inventory, Late Effects of Accidental Injury Questionnaire, General Health Questionnaire (GHQ-60) and two questionnaires for the general test of disaster effects.

The following statistical procedures were used: ANOVA (2 tests, discrimination analysis and linear correlation).

25% of the subjects did not answer questions about their dreams, 15% claimed they did not dream at all.

In the group of somatically traumatised subjects at war and in peacetime, there were significantly more dreams about the war and the old homeland, and significantly more dreams with negative emotions. Negative emotions were more present in the dreams of women and single subjects. The somatically traumatised subjects also had fewer dreams with collective symbols.

Dreams related to trauma, war and old homeland negatively correlate with the general neuroticism and with PTSD symptoms. General neuroticism correlated negatively with the series of dreams.

The obtained results were compared to the results of similar studies of other authors.

At the end, we presented a description of the dreams of both somatically traumatised and somatically non-traumatised subjects.

III

Studies of psycho(patho)logical state of refugees and somatically traumatised subjects

1. Research of psycho(patho)logical effects of refugeeism

Introduction: refugees in refugee camps

It is widely believed that 95% of the refugees in Serbia and Montenegro live in so-called family accommodation, while 5% live in collective camps (Rudić et al. 1994, Jovanović 1997, Opalić 1999, Čavić 2000). However, according to the latest sociological research (Ilić 2001), as many as 20% of refugees live in refugee camps today, 54% live at their relatives and friends' homes, while 20% of them have managed to provide their own dwelling place, and, in the majority of cases, food.

A special problem, as in all disasters, is posed by the elder population, comprising 13-15% of the refugee population (Nikolić-Balkoski et al. 2002), while among those in refugee camps the percentage is even higher, which results from the selection of younger and healthy refugees who manage to integrate in Serbia and Montenegro, move to other countries, or, in the lowest percentage of cases, return to the homelands they were expulsed from. The percentage of somatically ill and percentage of war invalids is, due to the same negative selection, higher in refugee camps.

A refugee collective functions to a great extent as a community, namely a group of people socially and emotionally inter-connected, like a rural community and in certain aspects like a family. Unfortunately, it rather often nurtures the so-called »exile culture« (Arenas 1996, Čavić 2002), or the »disaster subculture«, as named by the World Health Organisation (WHO 1992), in which the threshold of vulnerability related to the events experienced as jeopardising is lowered. The disaster subculture is marked by a prevailing passive attitude in coping with disaster effects and a more frequent and long-lasting symptom reaction to disaster, such as confusion, shock or disinhibited social behaviour.

Sociologist Lemert would speak of the secondary labelling of victims when a sufferer begins to feel as a victim in every situation – in other words, permanently introjects the transitional label of a traumatised refugee.

Therefore, no »salutary« (as termed by Schade, Schunk and Schüffel, 1998), i.e. healthful factors, activity capacities, optimism, call for receiving information and community support acceptance, including engagement in the support, are fully expressed in refugee camps, as the so-called pathogenic life factors – including, according to the above-mentioned authors, primarily unpreparedness for the stressful situation, then the lack of adequate social integration, and, finally, the culmination of all previous unpleasant events in one's life – prevail.

It should be noted that refugee camps are situated outside towns and operate in conditions that could be best described as semi-ghetto, thus disabling contacts of refugees with immediate neighbours or rendering them rather rare. The overall population, as emphasised by Ilić (2001), takes them as rivals in their own poverty, without any noticeable ethical solidarity, which is expectable considering the homogenous nationality of the refugees and the surrounding population. Accommodation conditions in camps (just to state it here – the euphemism »camp« is more often used in literature, so as to avoid a much closer-to-reality term »concentration camp«, as it arouses many negative associations) are very poor – for example, in the concentration refugee camp Krnjača, near Belgrade, on the way to Pančevo. The camp is comprised of workers' huts with primitive sanitary systems, in which several-generation refugee families live in a single room. Many of them have experienced transfer from one camp to another several times so far. These people are mainly of urban origin, with secondary school qualifications; less than half of them have employment, only 3% permanently. As many as one third of refugees live on humanitarian aid only, almost the same number solve their health-related problems - including, of course, mental ones - by applying self-medication (Čavić 2000).

The general climate in any refugee camp, although not devoid of solidarity, is characterised by animosity and quarrels, during which differences are emphasised rather than similarities. Briefly, the atmosphere prevailing in refugee camps is overburdened by the proneness of their inhabitants to making up their life balances, as well as with sub-depressive moods (low self-esteem, the experience of helplessness, dependency on other people, the impression of isolation, rejection or the experience of being neglected by relatives, community, society and even mankind).

Aims and hypotheses of the research

The main focus of the study is in determining certain mental, family and psychopathological features of subjects with a seven-year refugee status on the average, living in a refugee camp near Belgrade – in comparison to the somatically traumatised and subjects without trauma experience whatsoever.

The general aim of the research is to register the general mental integrity of the subjects with longer refugee status in refugee camps in comparison to some other groups at risk, or non-refugees in general. In other words, the main aim of the study is to determine the effects of refugeeism on the mental state in general, as well as the interdependence between these effects and certain measurable social and other relevant variables which we were able to control during our research and which, according to other authors, could influence them.

The aims of the research in a narrower sense, on the other hand, were as follows:

1. to determine the correlation between general neuroticism on one side and refugee status on the other, as refugees are expected to be more neurotic in comparison to the remaining population;
2. to determine the degree of burden of PTSD symptoms, as we supposed that, considering the acuteness of the injury, they are the most present in the group of somatically traumatised;
3. to discover the correlation between possible neuroticism features and burden of PTSD symptoms in traumatised subjects and refugees on one side, and their willingness to actively face negative effects of their trauma on the other;
4. to determine the correlation between basic features of refugees, e.g. trauma types, on one side, and the ways of coping with trauma effects on the other. We suppose that an active attitude in coping with negative effects of refugeeism is in positive relation with a higher degree of family cohesiveness, with a lower degree of psychopathological changes presence, as well as with younger age and higher qualifications of refugees;
5. to investigate the correlation between extroversion and introversion features with psychopathological status and other features of our subjects. We expect that more extrovert, rather than introvert, personalities would change their mental integrity less, since they are more willing, compared to introvert ones, to speak of their mental problem and thus increase the chances of solving it;
6. to determine the degree of family cohesiveness of our subjects, primarily refugees, in relation to non-refugees. The experience of family cohesiveness is in negative correlation with the overall neuroticism of refugees and other subjects, since it is generally known as a salutary factor.
7. to determine the correlation between socio-demographic features of our subjects and their mental integrity. More psychopathological features are expected among the elderly, those who are not married, live alone, and among subjects of lower education, than in their socio-demographic opponents.

Research method

a) Research sample

The sample is comprised of 284 subjects and divided into two main groups: experimental – 109 refugees living in refugee camp in Krnjača –, and a control group of non-refugees, divided into two sub-groups of subjects living in Belgrade. The first sub-group – 70 of them – are somatically traumatised patients of the Orthopaedic Hospital of the University Clinical Centre, Belgrade, while the second subgroup comprises 105 subjects from Belgrade denying any traumatic experience whatsoever. Table 11 shows the overall sample with its socio-demographic features.

Table No. 11. Socio-demographic features of refugee and non-refugee sample

SOCIO-DEMOGRAPHIC FEATURE		GROUPS OF SUBJECTS							
		REFUGEES		NON-REFUGEES				TOTAL	
				somatically traumatised		non-traumatised			
		f	%	f	%	f	%	f	%
Sex	Male	56	51.4	45	64.29	50	47.62	151	53.17
	Female	53	48.6	25	35.71	55	52.38	133	46.83
	20 years and less	11	10.1	10	14.29	16	15.24	37	13.03
	21-30 years	23	21.1	11	15.71	28	26.66	62	21.83
	31-50 years	34	31.2	27	38.57	49	46.67	110	38.73
	50 years and over	41	37.6	22	31.43	12	11.43	75	26.41
Marital status	Married	73	67.0	32	45.71	58	55.24	163	57.39
	Not married	36	33.0	38+	54.29	47	44.76	121	42.61
Family status	Living alone	12	11.0	22	31.43	38	36.19	72	25.35
	Living with partner/family member	97	89.0	48	68.57	67	63.81	212	74.65
Education	Elementary	21	19.3	16	22.86	5	4.76	42	14.79
	Secondary	70	64.2	38	54.28	58	55.24	166	58.45
	College & university degree	18	16.5	16	22.86	42	40.00	76	26.76

b) Research instruments

Beside the questionnaire on socio-demographic features of subjects, four standardised instruments were also applied, two of which investigate possible psychopathological change in refugees and other subjects, primarily those of neurotic character. The third instrument tests family homogeneity of subjects, while the fourth investigates the general attitude of subjects in coping with trauma effects.

1. PTSD-10 scale or Posttraumatic Stress Disorder Scale, instrument consisting of 10 questions, was prepared back in 1989 (Raphael, Lundin, Weisaeth). The total score of subjects, ranging from 0 to 20, is here used to estimate the degree of PTSD symptoms' presence, rather than for the purposes of diagnosing PTSD as such according to ICD-10 criteria.

2. Brief Eysenck's Personality Inventory, consisting of 15 variables, enables insight into two dimensions of personality - firstly, the dimension of general neuroticism, and secondly, extroversion and introversion dimension. Values attained are read in such a way that »No« answers get 2, and »Yes« answers 1 point each.

3. Family Homogeneity Index (FHI) (Mac Cubin 1991, according to Jovanović 1997), with 19 variables, was used in such a way that the total score value was treated as the measure of estimation of the emotional connection of our subjects with their families on the whole.

4. Impact of Events Scale with 15 variables testing two basic ways of coping with disaster effects: active (with 5 questions) and passive attitude (with as much as 10 items). Some researchers (Jovanović A. et al., 1997) also name them the imposition scale (active attitude) and avoidance scale (passive atti-tude).

c) Statistical data processing

In accordance with the research aims and the sample nature, the adequate statistical procedure was applied in our research. Since it is related to determining statistical significance in comparison of two or more arithmetic mean values of several sample features, the analysis of variances (ANOVA) was applied.

The procedure as explained above was applied for determining both statistical sig-nificance of differences for the comparison of the impact of certain variables on psy-chopathological status within the experimental group of refugees (primarily determin-ing the impact of socio-demographic variables on (psycho)pathological state), and statistical significance of differences between the presence of variables (mainly of psychopathological character) within all three subgroups of subjects (refugees, somatically traumatised and subjects with no trauma experience whatsoever).

Research results

a) Correlations between socio-demographic features of refugees and their (psycho)pathological status

Investigation of the impact of socio-demographic variables (sex, marital status, educa-tion and family status) on the degree of neurotic reaction or the degree of presence of extrovert-introvert dimension, by the application of Brief Eysenck's Personality In-ventory, in relation to refugee population only, is presented in Table No. 12.

Table No. 12. Values of statistically significant differences in the presence of certain psychopathological (neuroticism and PTSD symptoms), as well as psychological features (family cohesiveness, extroversion-introversion and active or passive attitude in coping with disaster effects) in refugee population only, in relation to their socio-demographic features

SOCIO-DEMO-GRAPHIC VARIABLE	SOCIO-DEMOGRAPHIC VARIABLE FEATURE, SIGNIFICANTLY DIFFERENTIATING PSYCHOPATHOLOGICAL FEATURE	PSYCHO-PATHO-LOGICAL FEATURE	RESEARCH INSTRUMENT	"F" VALUES	VALUE OF STATISTICAL SIGNIFICANCE OF DIFFERENCES' LEVEL
Sex	male	neuroticism	Eysenck Personality Inventory	$F_{1.106} = 4.44$	p = 0.0374
		PTSD symptoms	PTSD-10 Scale	$F_{1.107} = 7.67$	p = 0.0066
Marital status	married	PTSD symptoms	PTSD-10 Scale	$F_{1.107} = 4.22$	p = 0.0422

b) Comparison of certain psychological and psychopathological features of the refugee and non-refugee population

We shall take a look at the sub-samples of refugees and non-refugees (somatically traumatised and non-traumatised) upon statistically verified significances of the differences concerning the presence of PTSD – symptoms, neuroticism, extroversion and experience of family cohesiveness within all three tested subgroups. The results of the statistical significance verification of those differences are presented in Table No. 13.

Table No. 13. Values of statistically significant differences between psychological (extroversion and family cohesiveness) and psychopathological variables (neuroticism and PTSD symptoms), within the three groups of the subjects (refugees, somatically traumatised non-refugees and non-traumatised non-refugees)

SUBJECT SUB-GROUP IN WHICH THE FEATURE IS MOST PRESENT	SUBJECT SUB-GROUP IN WHICH THE FEATURE IS LEAST PRESENT	MENTAL I.E. PSYCHO-PATOLOGICAL FEATURE	RESEARCH INSTRUMENT	"F" VALUES IN THE VARIANCE ANALYSIS	VALUE OF STATISTICAL SIGNIFICANCE DIFFERENCES' LEVELS
Refugees	Non-traumatised	PTSD-symptoms	PTSD-10 Scale	F2.281=11.88	p = 0.0000
Non-traumatised	Refugees	Neuroticism	Eysenck Personality Inventory	F2.271= 5.27	p = 0.0057
Non-traumatised	Refugees	Extroversion	Eysenck Personality Inventory	F2.270=13.92	p = 0.0000

Discussion

What is statistically more significant is that there are more neurotic males than females (according to Eysenck Personality Inventory). These results have been confirmed also by another instrument examining similar symptoms, i.e. on PTSD-10 scale (Table No. 12). The reason for such a result may be found in the fact that males lost more due to refugeeism than females, considering that they had lost their external social framework (job, home, social reputation), as more significant existence frameworks of mental integrity (compared to females who had been and still are more oriented towards family life and family support, which has been maintained also with non-refugees, according to this research).

Table No. 13 shows that the refugees, compared to other subjects, are also statistically significantly most overburdened with PTSD symptoms (the second place is taken by the somatically traumatised and the third by non-traumatised subjects). It is probably the case of chronic PTSD symptoms, the increase of which has also been noted in our population by other authors (Špirić et al. 2002), and which occurs in 50% of the patients previously suffering from acute PTSD. It is possible that beside PTSD, some of the subjects also suffered from other serious mental problems. However, in personal contact with the subjects, we did not observe this, and the results on the instruments offered did not imply such problems. PTSD symptoms as the most frequent ones have also been confirmed on the refugee population from Serbia by other authors (Dimitrijević, Rašković-Ivić, Velimirović, Banovac, Milovanović, Oklobdžija, 2002). These results are in favour of the conclusion that the refugee situation, i.e. the conditions of existential hopelessness, influences the refugees to be probably less handicapped by the intrusion symptoms (nightmares, wretched memories, and so on) and irritability symptoms (inadequate concentration, increased starting reaction, and so on), and significantly more by the social isolation symptoms (emotional dullness, decreased interest for usual activities and so on) within PTSD.

It is interesting that the »general neuroticism« feature from the Eysenck Personality Inventory is most present in the sub-group of the non-traumatised and least in the sub-group of refugee population. The explanation for such a result may probably be found in the fact that our whole population is neuroticised considerably, that is, in the fact that this instrument for personality research registers so-called classical symptoms of neuroticism (anxiety, depression, and so on) less included by the PTSD-10 Scale. These results are probably influenced by the result that extroversion is most found in the sub-group reporting no trauma experience. And it may, no doubt, be in positive correlation with the ability to observe and report deeper, less dramatic aspects of the mental life of subjects than PTSD symptoms.

More on the basis of clinical impression originating from therapeutic work with the refuges than on the basis of the results of our study, we also noticed many hidden or somatised forms of depressive symptoms which, to a certain extent, correspond to the estimations of other authors relating to the refugees' mental state in refugee camps in Serbia and Montenegro (Čavić, 2000, 2002, Dimitrijević et al., 2002), and world-wide (Priebe, Denis, 1998).

Evidently more significant presence of PTSD symptoms, and in fact aggressive behaviour among veterans five years after injuring and participation at war was found in the research of Hume and Summerfield (1994).

We also found out (Table No. 12) that married refugees, unlike those who are not married (unmarried, divorced or widowers), suffer from some PTSD symptoms significantly more frequently, which is truly an unexpected result as literature recognises (Opalić, 1990) that marital status »protects« from neurotic reactions, especially when males are concerned. The fact that we found more neurotic ones among those who are married may be attributed to the fact that these subjects belong to a relatively elderly population, more inclined to mental de-compensation in stressful situation than middle-aged and younger subjects.

Our results showing that male refugees and married ones more frequently react with PTSD symptoms are in collision with the results obtained by other researchers with a similar population (Jovanović, Pejović et al., 1996). We explained our results by the fact that the subjects belonged to an elderly population on average (almost 40% of refugees are over 50). Besides, they were mainly married, while younger ones, probably under the influence of war events and refugeeism, had obstacles in establishing families and were single.

We did not confirm the findings of some researchers, also one of our hypotheses, that older (Weine et al. 1998) and less educated (Anastasijević 1996) refugees more frequently use passive and/or regressive mental mechanisms in overcoming the consequences of a disaster, as well as that they suffer more frequently from serious mental disorders (Leposavić et al. 2002). The reason may be found in the brutal biological selection which is responsible for the survival of elderly refugee subjects who were mentally and physically healthier, having in mind that the mortality and suicidal rate with the refugees are several times higher in comparison to the same rates of the domicile population (Opalić 2000). As a matter of fact, our results are, to a certain extent, similar to those obtained by Drozdek (1997), with a similar refugee population from Bosnia and Herzegovina in the Netherlands, so that social factors influencing the mental life of refugees do not play either a protective or a risk role in the development of PTSD. In other words, the presence of those symptoms in refugees placed at the refugee camp for a longer period of time, independently of social protective measures, does not change their mental state essentially. That means that key stress occurrence had happened earlier and caused, in a certain part of population, long-term symptoms of PTSD, despite the changes in the environment the refugees live in.

It is interesting to mention that the experience of family cohesiveness in the refugee population does not significantly differ from the family cohesiveness experience of non-refugees. The explanation for these results may be in the fact that the refugees in refugee camps, although experiencing difficult dwelling conditions, live with the members of their families. The observations of other authors (Leposavić et al. 2002) who describe a series of disorders in refugee families are linked with a disrupted emotional correlation of the members of refugee families, followed by the signs of mutual support loss, excessive protection or disturbed communication in general.

Certain socio-demographic features did not influence either the differentiation of refugees concerning active and passive behaviour in overcoming the consequences of the refugeeism, or the differentiation of refugees in their experience of family cohesiveness, except for those refugees (not presented in Table No. 12) who experienced injury during the expulsion. A certain number of refugees who had been somatically traumatised during the expulsion, significantly more frequently use - even after six years of refugee status - a passive mechanism in adapting to exile (F $1.107 = 4.303$; p $= 0.0404$). Obviously, it is a cumulative action of stress, i.e. the refugee situation on one side and the action of physical trauma on the other, each from their side inhibiting the initiative of somatically injured refugees to experience themselves as a decisive factor in overcoming the consequences of their refugeeism.

Altogether, our research confirmed that refugeeism presented existential and social crises with unavoidable mental consequences in terms of a reaction with PTSD symptoms. Having in mind that the consequences of refugeeism depend on the degree of alleviating unpleasant experiences of refugees, the maintenance of interpersonal relations and the degree of maintenance of self-respect, according to psychologists (Vlajković 1997), the refugees involved in our study probably still suffer from chronic PTSD symptoms (especially males and married ones). Contrary to that, general neuroticism (probably of anxiety-depressive character) is present even more significantly in the general population, i.e. among the subjects denying any significant life trauma, having in mind a serious social crisis we have been facing for more than 10 years.

Conclusions

Refugees, in comparison to non-refugees, significantly more frequently reacted with PTSD symptoms, which was attributed to chronic PTSD, noticed by other authors investigating the same population.

It is interesting that there is more neuroticism (probably of anxiety-depressive type) registered with the subjects denying severe trauma experience. This was explained by the possibility of a general neuroticism of the overall population of this time we are living in, that is, the findings according to which, the same group of subjects is significantly more frequently extrovert, i.e. liable to show deep and subtly shaded symptoms of general neuroticism.

We did not confirm that elderly and less educated refugees reacted with psychopathological symptoms more often.

Among the refugees, males more significantly and more frequently reacted with PTSD symptoms and general signs of neuroticism (in comparison to physically injured subjects). The reason for such a result probably lies in the fact that men are, in their existential crisis, much more affected by their refugee status (defeat of their external social plan in the form of the loss of job, estate, house, social reputation and social power). Such a defeat affects males more than females because of the social role they have – females are more oriented towards emotional investments in the family.

The refugees who at the same time experienced somatic injuries are more inclined to passive reactions to their refugeeism.

It is interesting that married refugees reacted with PTSD symptoms more frequently, which implies that losses (material and human) influence the health of married individuals more destructively in comparison to single refugees. It is excluded that such findings result from the fact that a lot of young refugees (relatively healthier) experienced impediments in getting married due to their exodus, while elderly ones, naturally, experienced more loses in their lives.

Resume

Certain mental and psychopathological effects of refugee life were examined in the study. The study involved 109 subjects from the refugee camp in Krnjača – their reactions were compared to the same reactions of 70 somatically injured patients from the Orthopaedic Hospital of the Clinical Centre, Belgrade and subjects (105) from Belgrade denying any traumatic experience whatsoever.

Beside the questionnaire on socio-demographic features, the subjects were asked to provide answers to PTSD-10 scale, Brief Eysenck's Personality Inventory, Family Homogeneity Inventory and Impact of Events Scale. By the implementation of appropriate statistical procedures (variance analysis), the significance of the differences among certain features within the experimental group of the refugees was examined, as well as the difference concerning the presence of mental and psychopathological features among all three subjects' sub-groups.

It was determined that, within the refugee group, males more significantly and more frequently reacted with PTSD symptoms, as well as with signs of general neuroticism, while married refugees more frequently reacted with PTSD symptoms.

In comparison to non-refugees, refugees are more significantly and more fre-quently handicapped with PTSD symptoms, which probably poses an expression of PTSD chronicity in this category of subjects.

Subjects who denied any significant traumatic experience in their lives mostly re-acted with the symptoms of general neuroticism, which is an interesting result which may be explained by the fact that the same group achieved the highest values on the extroversion scale (according to the same Eysenck instrument), or may be correlated to the increase of neurotic reactions in the whole population of Serbia and Montene-gro.

The mentioned and other results were comparable to the findings of similar re-searches performed by other authors.

2. Research of the Psychopathological State of Somatically Traumatised Subjects

Introduction

The interest in the consequences of somatic traumatisation has been of recent date only to those uninformed of the matter. The works dealing with this subject, though in general outline, could be found in the immediate aftermath of World War II. Ships J. G. and Coburn F. E. (1945), for instance, report on the so-called war neurosis (neurosis of war veterans), pointing out that it is related to many factors, among which individual ones are the most prominent.

This study is an attempt to discover what psychosomatics in a broader clinical sense does anyway - to shed more light on certain psychological and psychopathological phenomena related to the so-called objective pathological somatic phenomena and to establish the relationship between serious somatic injuries and potentially unhealthy psychological responses to such injuries. This study, therefore, focuses on the investigation of the so-called subjective consequences of somatic traumatisation – that is, on what happens to the somatically injured, not immediately following the accident when the injured is in a state of shock, pain-ridden and flooded with toxins, but several months after the injury took place.

In accordance to the World Health Organization recommendations on the investigation of psychosocial consequences of an accident, this study meets the demand to involve a control group in a two-fold way: subjects with mental trauma and subjects without any experience of trauma whatsoever are included in the study. The study is also related to the consequences of two, out of seven, key issues put forth by the WHO (1992) recommendations on trauma research. In other words, our study is related to distinguishing between the personal experience of facing trauma and the collective experience of trauma, as well as to indirect effects of certain therapeutic procedures (in this case the effects of surgical interventions on the injured at an orthopaedic ward).

The investigations of the psychological state following somatic trauma, as Feiereis (1983) writes, aims to discover potential neuroticism and other mental disorders which can be triggered or partially caused by a somatic injury. Putting it in contemporary terms, somatic trauma is in this paper investigated as a potential factor for the development of PTSD or some of the symptoms considered part of PTSD clinical state. (However, it has to be noted that PTSD Scale is used in this paper only to determine linear differences in the presence of PTSD symptoms in certain subgroups of our subjects, but not for a definite PTSD diagnosis, as done by the criteria of the International Classification of Diseases – ICD-DSM-III-R (WHO 1992).

This study also investigates the differences between the consequences of stress triggered by somatic trauma and mental trauma that some of the subjects experienced. In an indirect way the research also investigates the general level of stress in Serbia – the country which was under UN sanctions for 5 years (the sanctions resulted in restricted foreign trade affairs, no access to international funds and business transactions, limited travelling to foreign countries, and, finally and most important of all, a dramatic drop in living standards – by almost 300% in comparison to 1990). What we have in mind in particular is the fact that even that part of the control group, without ever having experienced any trauma, was living in such social circumstances that they may be considered stressful, especially compared to those of 8 years ago. WHO recommendations point out that the criteria of what is considered a disaster or stress in these countries have been constantly changing, i.e. dramatically reducing – this aspect of WHO recommendations probably refers to our sample.

Our intention is also to find out how certain aspects of trauma (e.g. amputation or inability to walk) as well as hospitalisation itself and the severity of injury influence the psychological condition. In other words, we wanted to determine, similarly to some authors (Bärbel, 1998; Feinstein, Dolan, 1991), if our patients respond to various kinds of somatic traumas (somatic traumas at war, in peacetime or somatic traumas in general) differently, depending on their social features.

Of course, the relations this research determines are not of a causal nature, since the research aims at establishing some general relations between certain phenomena and features of the subjects in relation to a series of circumstances, including the so-called trauma preconditions. The latter mainly refers to the mental and general health of the subjects prior to traumatisation, while the conditions of traumatisation refer to the features of accident referred to as important by the authors dealing with the issue (Schüffel, 1987; Raphael, Lundin, Weisaeth, 1989; WHO 1992) are talking about the preparedness for trauma (surprise factor), the experience of life jeopardy (the degree of trauma intensity experience), the experience of close persons' death in the same disaster, the loss of home, property, etc.

The studies dealing with the issue also analyse the ways of coping with trauma (Schunk, Schade, Schüffel, 1998; Berger, 1997; Solomon, Mikulincer, 1987) primarily in relation to the issue of active and passive attitude in coping with the accident.

Rather few related research works (Jovanović, 1997; Mitić, 1997) address the problem of a psychopathological response to traumatisation in family milieu, while family cohesiveness is considered a salutary, i.e. healthful factor in the prevention of psychic de-compensation of subjects under various types of stress (Schunk, Schade, Schüffel, 1998).

Sample

The total sample consisted of 175 subjects of different age, gender, marital status and professions. Out of the total number of subjects, 70 patients, hospitalised at the Orthopaedic Hospital of the University Clinical Centre, Belgrade in the course of 1998, comprised the experimental group. The experimental group was divided into two subgroups. The first subgroup (E_1) consisted of 26 persons traumatised during the war in Bosnia and Herzegovina, chiefly coming from the Serb Entity of B&H (The Republic of Srpska). Following their injury at the front or in the war area, they were sent away for treatment after having received first aid or having undergone casualty surgery intervention at the very spot. The fact is that among them there were more of those with sub-acute injury – the injury received up to two months prior to our research.

The second subgroup (E_2) consisted of 44 inhabitants of Belgrade and its vicinity, traumatised in peacetime, mainly injured at their workplace, in their spare time or in traffic accidents.

The control group consisted of 105 subjects, Belgrade residents, who were tested in 1998, either at their homes or at their workplaces (employees of the Railway Company, an institute's administrative staff, and a smaller group of randomly chosen acquaintances of the researchers). Exactly 45 of them had experienced trauma in their lifetime (mainly mental), whereas 60 of them stated that they had never had any trauma of somatic or mental nature whatsoever.

Table No. 14 shows the total sample and its socio-demographic features, expressed in frequencies and in the percentage of certain features' presence in all four subgroups.

The sample was rather uniform, to the extent allowed by the nature, that is, the character of such a research. In other words, the statistics showed that apart from gender, no other differences in the presence of certain socio-demographic features between four subgroups of subjects (E_1, E_2, K_1, K_2) existed.

It actually means that the uniformity in age among all four subgroups was attained. The predominating number of subjects were aged between 31 and 50, which is quite understandable since they comprise the population segment in its prime. Therefore, they were the population drafted for war and exposed to various injury risks.

The uniformity of gender was achieved in three subgroups, as men prevailed in the experimental subgroup involving war injuries, which is understandable since women were not being drafted.

There are no significant statistical differences regarding marital status of the subjects (»married« or »not married«) in all the four subgroups of the sample. The same is valid for their family status.

As for religious affiliation, the majority of our subjects declared themselves Orthodox Christians. The rest of them declared themselves either atheist or abstained from answering the question, probably considering it either superfluous or inappropriate (probably due to half a century of Communist atheism imposed on the Serb entity).

Table No. 14: Socio-demographic features of the sample

SOCIO-DEMOGRAPHIC FEATURES OF SUBJECTS			SUBGROUPS OF SUBJECTS				Total
			Experimental (E)		Control (K)		
			Somatic trauma at war (E₁)	Somatic trauma in peacetime (E₂)	Mental trauma only (K₁)	No mental nor somatic trauma (K₂)	
Gender	male	f (%)	25 (14.3)	20 (11.4)	23 (13.2)	27 (15.4)	95 (54.3)
	female	f (%)	1 (0.6)	24 (13.8)	22 (12.4)	33 (18.9)	80 (45.7)
Age	up to 20	f (%)	3 (1.7)	7 (4.0)	1 (0.6)	5 (2.8)	16 (9.1)
	21-30	f (%)	8 (4.6)	3 (1.7)	17 (9.7)	11 (6.3)	39 (22.3)
	31-50	f (%)	13 (7.4)	14 (8.0)	20 (11.4)	29 (16.6)	76(93.4.)
	over 50	f (%)	2 (1.1)	20 (11.4)	7 (4.0)	5 (2.8)	44 (25.2)
Marital - status	married	f (%)	9 (5.1)	23 (13.2)	26 (14.9)	30 (17.1)	88 (50.3)
	not married	f (%)	20 (11.4)	20 (11.4)	19 (10.9)	28 (16.0)	87 (49.7)
Family status	single	f (%)	12 (6.8)	10 (5.7)	12 (6.8)	26 (14.7)	60 (34.3)
	partner	f (%)	0 (0)	2 (1.1)	4 (2.3)	4 (2.3)	10 (5.7)
	partner and children	f (%)	6 (3.4)	19 (10.9)	19 (10.9)	20 (11.4)	64 (36.6)
	extended family	f (%)	8 (4.6)	13 (7.4)	1.0 (5.7)	10 (5.7)	41 (23.4)
Religious affiliation	Orthodox Christian	f (%)	9 (5.1)	18 (10.3)	38 (21.7)	43 (24.6)	108 (61.7)
	atheist	f (%)	4 (2.3)	13 (7.4)	2 (1.2)	10 (5.7)	29 (16.6)
	undeclared	f (%)	13 (7.4)	13 (7.4)	5 (2.9)	7 (4.0)	38 (21.7)
Profession	retired	f (%)	0 (0)	14 (8.0)	2 (1.1)	2 (1.1)	18 (10.3)
	blue-collar workers	f (%)	8 (4.6)	12 (6.9)	5 (2.8)	5 (2.8)	30 (17.1)
	experts	f (%)	1 (0.6)	4 (2.3)	20 (11.4)	29 (16.6)	54 (30.9)
	high-school & univ. students	f (%)	0 (0)	5 (2.8)	1 (0.6)	8 (4.6)	14 (8.0)
	other professions	f (%)	4 (2.3)	4 (2.3)	5 (2.8)	4 (2.3)	17 (9.7)
	undeclared	f (%)	13 (7.4)	5 (2.8)	12 (6.8)	12 (6.8)	42 (24.0)
Education	elementary	f (%)	0 (0)	11 (6.3)	1 (0.6)	1 (0.6)	13 (7.4)
	secondary	f (%)	12 (6.9)	11 (6.3)	20 (11.4)	23 (13.1)	66 (37.7)
	college & university degree	f (%)	1 (0.6)	11 (6.3)	18 (10.3)	29 (16.5)	59 (33.7)
	undeclared	f (%)	13 (7.4)	11 (6.3)	6 (3.4)	7 (4.0)	37 (21.1)

Concerning the profession, the white-collar subjects were more present in the control group and the blue-collar ones in the experimental group, which resulted from the fact that it was rather difficult to obtain a sample with a higher rate of blue-collars in Belgrade, which, being the capital of FR Yugoslavia, is more of an administrative and cultural, than industrial centre of the country.

As for three features: religious affiliation, profession and education, the percentage of undeclared (15-20%) is rather noticeable, being most probably the consequence of a certain ambivalence or treating these features as irrelevant by some of our sub-jects, taking the basic aim of the research into consideration.

In the final data processing, we also re-coded family status features, reducing them to only two options: »living alone« and »not living alone«.

Table No. 15 shows some clinical and situational features of the experimental group sample we could determine objectively, and which we believed to have certain influence on the psychopathological response of our subjects.

Table No. 15: Some clinical features of experimental group (70 subjects)

		CLINICAL FEATURE																CIRCUM-STANCES OF INJURY			
		the injured part of body			ampu-tation		difficult surgery		mobile		injury acu-teness		insom-nia		anti-depre-ssants treat-ment		anxio-lytic treatme nt					
		trunk	arms	legs	yes	no	yes	no	yes	no	yes	no	yes	no	yes	no	yes	no	at workplace	in traffic accident	in leisure time	at war
THE VALUE OF CLINICAL FEATURE	f	8	23	39	3	67	45	25	56	14	40	30	11	59	2	68	33	37	8	15	26	21
	%	11.4	32.9	55.7	4.3	95.7	64.3	35.7	80.0	20.0	57.1	42.9	5.7	84.3	2.9	97.1	47.1	52.9	11.4	21.4	37.1	30.0

Objectives and hypotheses

The main focus of our research was on determining potential psychopathological consequences of higher-degree somatic trauma demanding hospitalisation of subjects. However, the research, in an indirect way, also analysed the psychopathological con-sequences of life under stressful conditions, since all subjects included into the study originated from the country that had been living in a state very similar to the state of emergency.

Precisely, the objectives of the research are the following:

- to determine psychopathological change in the somatically and mentally traumatised, depending on their age, gender, profession and other socio-demographic features. We supposed that women, younger and elderly sub-jects, and possibly some other demographic categories of our subjects, were psychologically more sensitive to traumas;

- to determine possible psychopathological states among the somatically and mentally traumatised subjects, depending on the outer conditions of trauma-tisation. We supposed that psychological consequences of somatisation were more evident among the somatically traumatised at war, in comparison to the somatically traumatised in peacetime, i.e. that somatic injuries resulted in more diverse consequences that those resulting from mental trauma;

- to study the specificity of psychopathological change of our subjects in relation to the part of their bodies injured in trauma (legs, arms, trunk) and in relation to the acuteness of trauma, that is, if trauma was acute (experienced within a month of the research) or sub-acute (experienced a month or more prior to the research). We supposed that more recent traumas, and those affecting those body parts of more importance to the existence of subjects, result in more serious psychopathological changes of the traumatised;

- to attempt to determine in what way certain characteristics of somatic trauma (determined seriousness of surgery, possible amputation of a body part or inability to walk or move certain body parts) influence the subjects' psychopathological mode of responding. We supposed that the characteristics of more serious injuries of various natures result in more serious psychopathological changes;

- to determine the psychopathological state of the somatically and mentally traumatised, depending on the presence of certain predisposing variables existing even prior to the stress, e.g. earlier mental illness, general state of health or permanent personality features of the subjects (extroversion – introversion), the features which have already been determined by various authors to be related to psychological response to trauma;

- to determine the consequences of somatic and mental traumatisation on the psychological status of the subjects in relation to their preparedness for the trauma, which, we supposed justly, has negative correlations with the degree of psychopathological change;

- to determine the consequences of somatic and metal traumatisation on the psychological status of subjects in relation to psychosocial conditions of traumatisation and accompanying stressful moments (the factor of co-morbidity) such as the death of other persons with the same trauma, the experience of a life threat, the loss of home, etc., which, we supposed, should increase the possibility of more complex and more extensive psychopathological response;

- to study the psychopathological response of the somatically and mentally traumatised depending on family support, i.e. their family cohesiveness, which was, by various studies related to the issue, confirmed to decrease the possibility of psychopathological response – the supposition we also made;

- to determine the consequences of somatic and mental traumatisation on the psychological status of subjects depending on their active or passive attitude in coping with the trauma, that is, depending on the perception of their role and the importance of other people in their coping with traumatisation effects.

Research Instruments

All subjects were offered a set of research instruments – questionnaires. With prior brief explanation of the method of answering items, the questionnaires were given to the subjects to be filled in anonymously and without time limit for testing. The subjects were also informed that the questionnaires were not made up as a diagnostic procedure, but for scientific research purposes only. We assume that this resulted in some subjects remaining undeclared, especially in relation to their profession, education and religious affiliation, which is understandable, since those subjects, mainly serious somatic patients, were still under a strong impression of the surgical procedure they had recently undergone. For the same reason, that is, due to the most probably decreased concentration of our subjects, the offered Plutchik Test (PIE) remained unanswered in more than a third of all supplied questionnaires, which made us decide not to include it in our final data processing.

Concerning the choice of instruments, we strove to chiefly use those already used in other research of similar character.

In total, 337 variables were examined. The variables were used in various ways, either individually or within the summary result of a single instrument, or within a particular instrument of the summarised set of variables, and thus brought into relation with other features of the sample. Most of the variables were dichotomous, but some of them also offered as many as 12 answers (e.g. regarding profession).

We shall present the instruments in the sequence they were offered to the subjects and entered into the SPSS/W computer programme:

1) History – past experience – consisting of 25 variables, i.e., anamnestic data about the subjects. Those were the socio-demographic characteristics of the subjects (age, gender, profession) but also the experience of the accident and some aspects of trauma development. That one, as well as several other instruments, was taken from a widely known study by Raphael, Lundin, Weisaeth (1989).

2) Impact of Events Scale with 15 variables testing two out of three basic symptoms of Posttraumatic Stress Disorder. We took two variables from this scale: »active attitude in coping« (arrived at by summing up the replies to five questions) and »passive attitude in coping« (arrived at by summing up as many as 10 items from the questionnaire). Some researchers (Jovanovic et al., 1997) used this instrument in a similar manner, dividing it into two sub-scales: imposition scale and avoidance scale.

3) PTSD-10 scale or Posttraumatic Stress Disorder Scale was also used in the above-mentioned study (Raphael, Lundin, Weisaeth, 1989). It consists of ten items with

dichotomous answers. The result attained by the application of this instrument was calculated both summarily and linearly, and the differences related to the achievement on this instrument were determined on the basis of the total score on this instrument ranging from 0 to 20. (The concept of the instrument is such that higher values indicate a higher degree of mental health, whereas lower values point to the higher presence of PTSD.) In other words, we did not use this instrument for diagnostic purposes, because we did not, through personal contacts with the subjects, arrive at the conclusion that any of them, according to the criteria of the ICD-X International Diseases Classification (WHO, 1992), were suffering from PTSD.

4) Family Homogeneity Index (FHI) (Jovanović, 1997), with 19 variables, was applied to investigate the relationship between the cohesiveness of a family system on one side, and the effects and other aspects of the accident (preparedness, the way of coping with stress) on the other. The results of all the instrument items were used in such a way that the total instrument score was utilised.

5) Brief Eysenck's Personality Inventory, with 15 variables, has been applied in a series of studies related to this issue. It enables insight into two dimensions significant to coping with stress. Firstly, it is the dimension of extroversion and introversion, and then there is the dimension of neuroticism, which is indispensable in the psychopathological evaluation of accident effects on a subject's psychological state. (Values attained were read in such a way that a »No« answer got 2 and a »Yes« answer got 1 point; i.e. lower absolute values indicated a higher presence of a particular feature.)

6) General Accident Questionnaire was taken from the above-mentioned research. With 28 items, it tests various accident aspects (preparedness for the accident, traumatic experience intensity, accident duration, the loss of close persons and property in the accident). The answers to separate questions were calculated separately, i.e., as separate variables.

7) What have you done to cope with the accident effects? is an instrument consisting of 12 items. It was also taken from the above-mentioned research and represents a more extensive and somewhat repeated investigation of coping with psychological and objective problems related to the accident.

8) Late Effect of Accidental Injury Questionnaire (LEAIQ), proposed by some authors (Raphael, Lundin, Weisaeth, 1989), refers to a comprehensive investigation - 76 variables. It partly coincides with the question contents of the above instruments. However, it bears a somewhat higher specific significance since its questions refer to a series of experiences during the accident, the circumstances of its occurrence and other trauma aspects (relevant to the goals of our research) six months after the accident occurred. Therefore, this questionnaire investigates the late psychological response to trauma. Due to the extensiveness of this detailed instrument, questions referring to psychological characteristics of neurotic response were summarised into cluster variables, therefore obtaining summary dependent variables, that is, the charac-

teristics of psychological response. They include: general neuroticism, depression, anxiety, neurotic somatisation, cognitive neurotic disorders and insomnia. These summary dependent variables consist of the answers to two – five questionnaire items.

9) General Health Questionnaire (GHQ-60) is related to mental health and is a rather extensive form - 60 variables - of instrument devised to investigate general mental health. (There is also a form consisting of 30 variables). This instrument was offered with the goal to verify, in a more objective way, the results obtained by applying some of the above-mentioned instruments. It was also applied in a number of other researches, whereas, in the present one, it was applied in such a manner that higher figures indicate a lower degree of mental maturity, and vice versa.

It should be noted that the control group subjects without the experience of somatic injury were offered all instruments except General Accident Questionnaire, What have you done to cope with the accident effects? and General Health Questionnaire (GHQ-60), since it was not necessary to research in such a detailed manner the conditions under which the accident happened, the features and consequences of the accident. In addition, their motivation to take part in our research was to a certain extent lower than among the subjects from the experimental group.

Statistical data processing

When the variables were categorical to determining their mutual relationship, that is, to verify the statistical significance of the differences in the presence of a particular feature of the subject (independent variables) depending on the particular aspects of psychical, that is, psychopathological state (dependent variables), Pearson's χ^2 test was used.

Pearson's r-coefficient - linear correlation coefficient - was used for defining the correlation between two interval variables, and interval and dichotomous variables.

A significant part of statistical data processing involved the verification of the significance of differences between the arithmetic mean values of almost all features' presence within the experimental group, that is, the differences between the features of the somatically traumatised at war and in peacetime (E_1 and E_2 sub-groups respectively).

However, the focus of statistical data processing was placed on comparing the quality and quantity of responses to trauma on one side and other features of the subjects on the other between all four subgroups simultaneously (between E_1, E_2, K_1 and K_2), which is understandable considering the character of our sample. The focus was on the statistical verification of the significance of certain dependent variables (the features of psychopathological state) in four subgroups in which independent variable – trauma, that is, its feature – was also present. However, the nature of certain de-

100

pendent variables demanded the verification of their being related to certain independent variables to be carried out in some additional combinations. The differences in the presence of a certain feature between E_1, E_2 and K_1 subgroups were tested (when the effects of differences between certain trauma types were examined). Therefore, the control subgroup of non-traumatised subjects was not included.

The differences in the presence of specific features (the features related to the presence of psychopathological specificity of somatic traumatisation in general) between the control and the experimental group (K and E) were also tested. Some features of the whole experimental group (E) were compared to the same features of the control group subgroups (K_1 and K_2), mainly when we aimed at a more differentiating analysis of what could influence the type and the intensity of the psychopathological response of somatically traumatised subjects. For the same reason, the significance of certain features, in comparing the whole experimental group and the control subgroup of subjects without the experience of trauma whatsoever (E and K_2), was researched.

Results and comments

We shall present the results of the research in aspects in which certain, more or less specific, features of our subjects, significant to their psychological response following their traumatisation, were verified.

Primarily, they include socio-demographic features (gender, age, marital status, education, profession and nationality), some individual predispositions (earlier psychological problems, earlier health problems, extroversion), war and peacetime conditions of traumatisation, the nature of somatic injury (the experience of trauma severity, mobility following the injury, the body part injured in trauma, the involvement of surgical procedure), traumatisation conditions (the experience of life threat, other persons' deaths, the loss of home and the like in the same trauma), family context of somatisation (family cohesiveness, the death of other family members and the like), preparedness for trauma, and the ways of coping with trauma (the time elapsed until first responses to trauma, passive or active attitude towards trauma, satisfaction with the provided care, and the like).

The results will be presented by presenting only those that were statistically confirmed to be significant in relation to their impact on the psychopathological status of the traumatised. For every narrower or wider psychopathological feature, the values of relevant statistical differences present in certain subgroups of subjects will also be presented. In other words, the very nature of psychopathological feature (dependent variable) was verified in several combinations related to subjects' features (independent variable).

101

We first calculated the scores whose statistical value was more significant. These include the total scores of the following instruments: Post Traumatic Stress Disorder Scale (PTSD-Scale), General (Mental) Health Questionnaire (GHQ-60), and Family Homogeneity Index (FHI). The dependent variables included total scores obtained within dimensions of neuroticism and extroversion – introversion from Short Eysenck Personality Inventory, then the total scores signifying passive and active attitude in coping with trauma effects from the Impact of Events Scale.

Dependent variables were also some psychopathological features comprised of 2-6 items from the Late Effect of Accidental Injury Questionnaire (LEAIQ) and General (mental) Health Questionnaire (GHQ-60). They include the following: depressed mood, anxiety, general neuroticism, neurotic cognitive disorders, insomnia, neurotic somatisation and paranoid experience. The variables, that is, certain psychopathological and other features related to the experience of trauma obtained by answers to a single question - item, were taken from these two questionnaires, as well as from the History.

The results will, for easy reference, be presented in tables along with the values of corresponding statistical procedures (variance analysis or χ^2 test, that is, linear correlation coefficient). Statistical levels of significance along with stating the subgroups included in the applied procedure will also be provided.

2.1 Socio-demographic features of the subjects and their psychopathological status

Table No. 16 shows the results of statistically confirmed narrower demographic features of the subjects with potential impact on their psychopathological responses.

As shown in the table, the religion of the subjects did not differentiate significantly from the psychopathological status of the subjects, which is quite understandable since the subjects were mainly Serb Orthodox Christians.

As for education, it was concluded that passive attitude in coping with trauma effects was significantly more present ($F_{2.43} = 3.38$; $p < 0.05$) in the subjects with elementary and secondary education. However, it is interesting that the subjects with elementary school only at the same time also had an active attitude towards coping with their problem. Having in mind that the subjects of secondary education significantly more often took a passive attitude in coping with trauma effects, it may be concluded that these subjects were more neurotically inhibited by somatic traumatisation than those of lower education, probably due to the fact that they could perceive the possible outcome of their injury better or due to a higher degree of professional frustration resulting from their physical injury. Moreover, the subjects of elementary education only were more somatisation-prone that the others, which has already been confirmed by studies dealing with social factors of neurotic response (Opalić 1990).

Table No. 16: Psycho(patho)logical features of subjects in experimental group (E) and the total sample (E+K) significantly differentiated in statistical sense by a narrower demographic feature

DEMOGRAPHIC FEATURE — wider demogr. feature	narrower demogr. feature significantly differentiating psycho-(pathol.) characteristic	PSYCHOPATHOLOGICAL FEATURE INCREASED IN TERMS OF STATISTICAL SIGNIFICANCE IN NARROWER DEMO-GRAPHIC FEATURE (THE INSTRUMENT IT WAS TAKEN FROM)	ARITHMETIC MEANS OF NARROWER DEMOGRAPHIC FEATURES	"F" VALUES FROM THE VARIANCE ANALYSIS	"P" VALUES	THE SAMPLE PART INCLUDED INTO THE ANALYSIS
Age	30 years and over	cognitive dysfunction(LEAIQ)	$AMV_{<20y}= 0.25$ $AMV_{21y-30y}=0.51$ $AMV_{31y-50y}=0.13$ $AMV_{>50y}=0.14$	$F_{3.171}=5.43$	p<0.01	E+K
Gender	female	insomnia (GHQ-60)	$AMV_m =14.47$ $AMV_f =17.08$	$F_{1.66}= 4.82$	p<0.05	E
	female	anxiety (GHQ-60)	$AMV_m = 1.89$ $AMV_f = 2.44$	$F_{1.68}= 5.86$	p<0.05	E
	female	paranoid experience (GHQ-60)	$AMV_m = 1.91$ $AMV_f = 2.52$	$F_{1.68}= 7.00$	p<0.05	E
	female	depressed mood (GHQ-60)	$AMV_m = 13.11$ $AMV_f = 16.08$	$F_{1.68}=7.18$	p<0.01	E
	female	extroversion (Eysenck Personality Inventory)	$AMV_m = 9.45$ $AMV_f =10.19$	$F_{1.59}=4.24$	p<0.01	E
	female	mental dysfunction (GHQ-60)	$AMV_m =122.87$ $AMV_f =146.20$	$F_{1.68}=10.94$	p<0.01	E
Marital status	single	PTSD (PTSD Scale)	$AMV_s = 16.86$ $AMV_f = 15.40$	$F_{1.60}=4.78$	p<0.05	E
	married	cognitive dysfunction (LEAIQ)	$AMV_n = 0.14$ $AMV_m = 0.36$	$F_{1.16}=7.49$	p<0.01	E+K
Educa-tion	elementary and secondary education	passive attitude in coping with trauma effects (Impact of Events Scale)	$AMV_m =10.45$ $AMV_s =10.13$ $AMV_{he} = 5.80$	$F_{2.43}=3.38$	p<0.05	E
	elementary education	active attitude in coping with trauma effects (Impact of Events Scale)	$AMV_e = 7.00$ $AMV_s = 4.09$ $AMV_{he} = 3.29$	$F_{2.135}=4.86$	p<0.01	E+K
	elementary education	somatisation (LEAIQ)	$AMV_{ee} = 1.08$ $AMV_s = 0.42$ $AMV_{he} = 0.31$	$F_{2.135}=5.68$	p<0.01	E+K
Family	single	neuroticism (Eysenck Personality Inventory)	$AMV_s = 14.78$ $AMV_{wf} = 13.99$	$F_{1.164}=4.49$	p<0.05	E+K
	with family	general neuroticism (LEAIQ)	$AMV_s = 0.33$ $AMV_{wf} = 0.61$	$F_{1.173}=5.37$	p<0.05	E+K
	with family	passive attitude in coping with trauma effects(Impact of Events Scale)	$AMV_s = 6.70$ $AMV_w = 6.97$	$F_{1.173}=6.10$	p<0.05	E+K

Marital status influences the psychopathological response in such a way that the subjects who were ›not married‹ achieved significantly higher scores on the PTSD Scale ($F_{1.60} = 4.78$; $p < 0.05$), probably due to the well-known mental protection family provides. Those who were ›married‹, however, expressed neurotically decreased cognitive functions (reduction in memory capacity and poor concentration abilities) in a statistically significant way ($F_{1.163} = 7.49$; $p < 0.01$), probably due to the fact that there were more elder subjects among them, in which the significantly higher presence of the psychopathological feature was statistically confirmed.

The variable of gender, however, differentiates a series of psychopathological variables (Table No. 19). It was statistically confirmed that women more significantly suffered from insomnia ($F_{1.68} = 4.82$; $p < 0.05$), anxiety ($F_{1.68} = 5.86$; $p < 0.05$), paranoid experience ($F_{1.68} = 7.00$; $p < 0.05$) and depression ($F_{1.68} = 7.18$; $p < 0.05$) in comparison to men. The result was also confirmed by the result arrived at on GHQ-60 Questionnaire, according to which, women showed statistically more significant worse mental health ($F_{1.68} = 10.98$; $p < 0.01$), which is not surprising since the aforementioned individually-taken psychopathological features were taken from GHQ-60. Concerning the feature ›insomnia‹, six items (all related to sleeping disorders) were used, for ›depression‹, five answers (related to hypersensitivity and changes of mood, apathy, the loss of self-confidence, the feeling of being worthless, and hopelessness). The feature ›suicidal thoughts‹ was comprised of four answers also taken from GHQ-60 (questions: whether the subject attempted suicide, wished he were dead, or had the idea of committing suicide, whether he had the feeling his life was worthless). ›Paranoid experience‹ was taken from the answers to only one GHQ-60 question related to the feeling of being watched by others or being convinced the others had something against him/her. The fact that women were significantly less present in the subgroup of traumatised at war, has a significant impact on the differences between psychopathological responses of subjects injured at war and in peacetime. Another feature characteristic of women, confirmed to be significantly more ($F_{1.59} = 4.24$; $p < 0.01$) present among them is extroversion – the readiness to speak of their unpleasant feelings in general and therefore also in a research. The latter result is well known to all psychotherapists – from their experience they know that women in a faster and easier manner perceive and speak of their negative feelings and seek aid in coping with them.

The demographic variable of family status (which we later on decoded into two: ›single‹ and ›not single‹) at the first glance pointed to a contradictory impact, significantly increased neuroticism among ›singles‹ (total score on Brief Eysenck Personality Inventory) and increased overall neuroticism (three items from LEAIQ related to statistically significant presence of the following symptoms: ›nervousness‹, ›weakness‹ and ›irritability‹) among those who are ›not single‹. Since standardised Brief Eysenck Personality Inventory is a more relevant instrument (comprised of as many as

9 items related to neuroticism), it can be concluded that according to our research, ›single‹ subjects are more neurotic. Moreover, this was confirmed by a series of other studies.

It is interesting that the subjects living in a family had a more passive attitude in coping with trauma effects, probably due to the support they received or expected from their family members.

Table No. 17 presents the results of calculations related to the potential impact of demographic variable – the age of our subjects – on their psychopathological and psychological features of response to somatic trauma.

Table No. 17: Statistically significant correlations between certain psycho(patho)logical features and the age of subjects within the experimental group (with somatic trauma)

PSYCHO(PATHO)LOGICAL FEATURE (THE INSTRUMENT IT WAS TAKEN FROM)	THE VALUE OF CORRELATION COEFFICIENT (R)		THE LEVEL OF SIGNIFICANCE OF CORRELATION COEFFICIENT (P)		CORRELATION DEGREE	
	injured at war	injured in peacetime	injured at war	injured in peacetime	injured at war	injured in peacetime
family cohesiveness(FHI)	-0.48		p< 0.01		*	
PTSD presence (PTSD Scale)	0.29		p< 0.05		*	
neuroticism (Eysenck Personality Inventory)	0.39		p< 0.01		*	
mental dysfunction, total score (GHQ-60)	0.42		p< 0.05		*	
depressed mood (GHQ-60)	0.45		p< 0.05		*	
paranoid experience (GHQ-60)	0.26		p = 0.056		statist. trend	
suicidal thoughts (GHQ-60)	0.51		p< 0.01		**	
Active attitude in coping with trauma effects (Impact of Events Scale)	-0.44		p< 0.05		*	
Passive attitude in coping with trauma effects (Impact of Events Scale)	-0.41		p< 0.05		*	

Left-side vertical labels: total score of a certain instrument; feature made up of several items of a certain instrument.

-r → predominantly in younger subjects (< 30yrs)
+r → predominantly in older subjects (> 30yrs)
*** = r = 0.70-0.90 = high correlation
** = r = 0.50-0.70 = medium correlation
* = r < 0.50 = low correlation

As for the age of the subjects included in our research, we concluded that younger traumatised subjects were extremely ambivalent in relation to their attitude in coping with trauma (see Table No. 16). Younger age of subjects significantly correlates (the correlation is truly low) with both an active and a passive attitude in coping with trauma effects. Let us just keep in mind that the variable ›active attitude in coping‹ consists of the answers to five items (›I tried to forget the accident‹, ›I avoided being

105

disturbed by the thought of the accident‹. ›I avoided everything that reminded me of the accident‹, »I tried not to talk about the accident‹, ›I endeavoured not to think of the accident‹). The variable ›passive attitude in coping with trauma‹ consisted of answers to 10 items (the questions were similar to the previous ones, but had a negation to them, with additional questions related to sleeping disorders, the contents of dreaming, the negation of daydreaming and being overwhelmed by dull feelings related to the traumatic experience).

The stated ambivalence of younger subjects included in our study is most probably the result of the optimistic attitude of the young and the energy (active attitude) younger people have on the one hand, and on the other (passive attitude), the increased support of family (significant correlations of the young age of subjects with the degree of family cohesiveness: r=-0.48). On the other hand, there is also the experience of a high degree of physical handicap, which is more painful at a younger age (although our research did not register it). Elderly subjects injured at war were significantly more often suicidal (average high correlation: r = 0.51), more depressive (r = 0.45) and more paranoid (truthfully speaking, only at the level of statistical trend). These results were also confirmed by the total score of the General (mental) Health Questionnaire GHQ-60, whose values show that during war, elderly somatised subjects are those who significantly more often de-compensate. GHQ-60 questionnaire is comprised of 60 questions, the positive answers of which in general refer to the presence of mental disturbances, so that the total GHQ score also indicates the degree of psychiatric disorder.

Table No. 16 also shows that elderly subjects somatically traumatised in peacetime decompensate significantly more often (low but statistically significant correlation) toward neurotic response, regardless of its being of reactive character (significantly higher values of PTSD) or of more lasting character (significantly higher values obtained on the neuroticism sale of Brief Eysenck Personality Inventory). All in all, the elderly subjects somatically traumatised in peacetime (probably due to general tendency towards neuroticism) respond with symptoms significantly more often than younger subjects. Since there were fewer elderly subjects in the subgroup of traumatised at war, it probably resulted in their not showing significantly more evident signs of a psychiatric disorder of depressive, suicidal or paranoid character. It may also result from the relatively cold response of the wider social community to their health-related problems. The wounded at that war were not treated as heroes in the Yugoslav public but barely as war veterans, and more often as unfortunate people who had had an accident at war.

It should be added that our data processing showed that other socio-demographic features did not differentiate any psychopathological features, individually or jointly taken, especially not those related to the conditions of traumatisation (the experience of severity of injury, the fact that a close person was killed or a home lost in the same

106

accident) and those related to pretrauma conditions (earlier psychological state of subjects and their preparedness for trauma).

2.2 Individual predispositions of subjects with potential influence on their psychopathological response to trauma

Primarily, this concerns the results obtained on Brief Eysenck's Personality Inventory extroversion-introversion scale, several items from LEAIQ questionnaire, and several features taken from other instruments related to earlier psychiatric problems and illness in general.

The issue of the subjects' psychiatric heredity was not raised, since we estimated that the proneness toward psychic disease in one's family was most usually denied by subjects included in poll researches. Sincere answers to such questions can be obtained, in our opinion, only if therapeutic relationship is established with a patient, trust gained and motivation increased to provide information on oneself causing minor narcissistic trauma.

In addition to the described feature of extroversion significantly more present in women of the experimental group ($F_{1.59} = 4.24$; $p < 0.01$), we did not discover any differences at the level of the total sample, not even when differences in the presence of this feature in all four subgroups were verified statistically. Neither were the differences found between groups related to their ›previous state of general health‹ (11 questions from the History).

However, determined were the differences ($\chi^2 = 13.43$: $p < 0.05$) in relation to ›earlier problems with nerves‹, less present in E_1 experimental subgroup (of traumatised during war) and K_2 control subgroup (stating no experience of trauma whatsoever). Generally more ›problems with nerves‹ had subjects traumatised in peacetime (E_2) but also mentally traumatised in peacetime comprising K_1 subgroup of the control group ($\chi^2 = 10.97$; $p < 0.05$). The result indirectly supports the thesis on accident-prone persons. Our research showed that some subjects with earlier psychological problems are traumatised (either somatically or mentally) even in peacetime. On the other hand, those most seriously injured, with somatic war trauma, although showing a high degree of psychopathological response, had had no ›problems with nerves‹ earlier in their lives. Such problems, when emerging later on, were most probably supported by factors accompanying somatic trauma at war (the loss of a close person, home or property in the same accident and the experience of a life threat). Kaličanin, Bjelogrlić, Petković (1992) carried out on the same Serb population, showed that in war conditions the most jeopardised (proneness to PTSD development or more severe mental illness) parts of population were already-registered psychiatric patients and members of their families, which partially corresponds to the results we obtained.

2.3 Psychopathological response depending on the type of traumatisation (physical, general, war, peacetime)

One of the key objectives of this research was to determine the impact of the variable of somatic injury inflicted in war conditions (at the frontline or in war areas) accompanied by a high degree of somatic injury probability, as well as by a high degree of psychological tension which, this way or another influences the psychological condition of somatically traumatised patients. A reliable reply to this question could be obtained only if the problem was analysed also in relation to the same or similar somatic traumas in peacetime, that is, in relation to general (most often mental) traumatisation, or more precisely, in comparison to the subjects from the same population who had no experience of mental of somatic trauma.

a) The results obtained from the total score of individually taken instruments in relation to the general psychological condition

One of the key results we obtained (see Table No. 18) reveals that the statistically more significant degree of PTSD appearance (PTSD Scale) appeared in the subgroup with somatic war trauma, in comparison to those somatically traumatised in peacetime. As a matter of fact, proneness towards response to trauma with PTSD symptoms was more present among all traumatised subjects (E_1, E_2 and K_1 subgroup) than among the non-traumatised ones (K_2), which is quite understandable.

By analysing the whole sample, we also arrived at the conclusion that there was a significantly higher degree of neuroticism (according to Eysenck's Inventory) in the somatically traumatised at peacetime and in healthy subjects in comparison to the other two subgroups (see Table No. 17). The result supports the conclusion that somatic traumas in peacetime pose a less serious threat to mental health than general trauma in one's life. In other terms, somatic war trauma, according to our research, takes the first place when PTSD-development risk is concerned. The findings, we suppose, are not related to the injury severity (since we did not establish such differences between the responses of the somatically traumatised at war and in peacetime). It is, likewise, not correlated to preparedness for accident (since it was significantly worse in the subgroup of traumatised in peacetime as well as in the control group: $\chi^2 = 33.61$; $p < 0.01$). It is most probably related to the fact that those traumatised at war at the same time significantly more often ($\chi^2 = 12.10$; $p < 0.01$) experienced a death of a close person during the course of the same war, and that at the moment of their injury, in comparison to other subjects, significantly more often ($\chi^2 = 17.83$; $p < 0.01$) thought of their own death, that is, were vitally threatened. The factor which could be called general exhaustion by war could also be considered.

Having in mind the highest values of Family Homogeneity Index, in the subgroup of those traumatised at war (see Table No. 18), it could be concluded that the injury contributed to the subject's family cohesiveness. It could result from the fact that these subjects were generally younger, since other researches (Jovanović 1997) arrived at the conclusion that a war invalid's family was far less homogenous that similar ones. Some other factors not analysed in our research may be responsible for such findings. A similar value of family cohesiveness ($F_{3.17} = 2.97$; $p < 0.05$) was also found only among K_2 subgroup of subjects experiencing no trauma whatsoever.

It is interesting that we did not establish any statistically significant differences in relation to the General Health Questionnaire in all four subgroups, which, to a certain degree, revitalises the above results, although when certain items are analysed separately, as we did later on, expected differences between psychopathological response of certain subgroups are confirmed.

What is very obvious is that we did not establish a significant presence of psychopathological response only among the subjects of K_2 subgroup without any traumatic experience, which was rather predictable.

Depressive response was distinguished mainly in both subgroups of those somatically injured (during war and peacetime), anxiety only in the subgroup of those mentally traumatised in peacetime (which was confirmed twice).

On the other hand, insomnia (in reality, very often present in depression but also in other forms of neurotic response) together with somatisation was present in all three subgroups of (both somatically and mentally) traumatised individuals.

General neuroticism was significantly distinguished in the subgroups of those traumatised in peacetime (K_1 and E_2), obviously regardless of the traumatisation type.

The results presented in Table No. 18 allow the conclusion that the mildest psychopathological response, anxiety, was the most present in those mentally traumatised in peacetime. Then follows an undefined symptom, general neuroticism, registered significantly in the subgroups of those traumatised in peacetime (both somatically and mentally) and psychogenic somatisation together with insomnia, which is the most widely present form of psychiatric response, highly present in all three subgroups of traumatised subjects. The most serious form of response, confirmed significantly among the somatically traumatised, is depressed mood, the only response present in both subgroups of the somatically traumatised (at war and peacetime).

The most differentiated form of group response, among subjects of our research, was anxiety, present more significantly only in one subgroup – the subgroup of the mentally traumatised in peacetime. Then follows depressed mood, which as a form of psychopathological response was distinguished in both subgroups of somatically traumatised subjects.

Table No. 18: Psychopathological and psychological features of traumatisation (obtained from the total score of certain instruments in certain subgroups) whose statistical presence is significantly increased

(E = E_1 + E_2 : E_1 – somatically traumatised at war, E_2 – somatically traumatised in peacetime)
(K = K_1 + K_2 : K_1 – mentally traumatised in peacetime, K_2 – no mental or somatic trauma whatsoever)

SUBGROUP OF SUBJECTS (E_1, E_2, K_1, K_2) IN WHICH THE PRESENCE OF A FEATURE IS SIGNIFICANTLY INCREASED	PSYCHO-(PATHO)LOGICAL FEATURE WHOSE STATISTICAL PRESENCE INSIGNIFICANTLY INCREASED	INSTRUMENT WHOSE TOTAL SCORE HAS BEEN CALCULATED	χ^2 TEST VALUES OR "F" FROM THE VARIANCE ANALYSIS	STATISTICAL SIGNIFICANCE OF DIFFERENCES LEVEL	THE SUBGROUPS INCLUDED INTO STATISTICAL DATA PROCESSING
E_1	proneness to PTSD	PTSD Scale	$F_{1,168}$ = 3.94	p<0.05	E_1+E_2
E_1+E_2+K_1	proneness to PTSD	PTSD Scale	$F_{1,173}$ = 15.27	p<0.01	E_1+E_2+K_1+K_2
E_1+K_1	neuroticism	Brief Eysenck Personality Inventory	$F_{3,162}$ = 6.45	p<0.01	E_1+E_2+K_1+K_2
E_1	family cohesiveness	FHI	χ^2 = 6.45	p<0.01	E_1+E_2+K_1+K_2

If we summarise psychopathological features obtained from several items, that is, from the total score of a single instrument within certain subgroups, their concentration among subjects traumatised at war can be observed, it should be emphasized, on the instruments from which the offered answers were used (twice on PTSD Scale and once on Eysenck's Personality Inventory). However, as far as psychopathological responses' concentration is concerned, those somatically traumatised in peacetime do not follow the traumatised at war, which could be expected considering the nature of their trauma (mainly difficult physical injury), but those mentally traumatised in peacetime.

In other words, the quantitatively most distinguished psychopathology, according to this methodology, was noticed in the subgroup with somatic war trauma (general proneness to neurotic response), and then, among those mentally traumatised in peacetime. The third place is taken by the somatically traumatised in peacetime, which means that the experience of physical injury in everyday life, generally speaking, causes milder psychopathological consequences even in comparison to an average (most often mental) trauma in one's life. However, this is not valid for war trauma, which, due to its stress-inducing nature and its consequences to mental health, obviously, takes the first place.

Summarising the symptoms of psychopathological response and severity of injury, it could be concluded that undefined traumas (general traumatisation in peacetime) are usually followed by anxiety, that medium-intensity traumas (physical traumas in peacetime) by insomnia, conversion symptoms and general neuroticism, while the most difficult traumas (physical traumas at war which correlate with the loss of a close person or property and the experience of life jeopardy) by depressed mood, which, as widely known, is a predictor of possible PTSD appearance among the afflicted.

b) The results obtained on the basis of several replies to items related to certain psychopathological feature

More qualitative investigations were performed by means of variables obtained by selecting certain items from the Late Effect of Accidental Injury Questionnaire (LEAIQ) and using groups of questions related to specific psychopathological entities. First of all, these were »insomnia«, consisting of two items (›nightmare experience‹ and ›sleep disorders‹), »depressed mood«, consisting of five items (›lack of initiative‹, ›changes of mood‹, ›decreased general capacity‹, ›depression experience‹ and ›fatigue‹), followed by »somatisation« or somatic problems of psychogenic origin also obtained from the answers to five questions (concerning ›vertigo‹, ›perspiration‹, ›indigestion‹, ›somatic pains not related to the injury‹, ›headache‹). The ensuing were: »anxiety«, consisting of four items (›fear or timidity‹, ›tension‹, ›fear of a situation similar to the accident‹, ›wincing at a sudden noise‹), »general neuroticism«, obtained from the answers to three questions (regarding ›irritability‹, ›general weakness‹ and ›nervousness‹), and finally, neurotic »cognitive disorders«, consisting of two items (›decreased capacity to memorise‹ and ›decreased capacity to concentrate‹).

As shown in Table No. 19, the concentration of psychopathological response is more present among people who experienced trauma in various conditions. What is striking is the fact that we did not determine a significant presence of psychopathological response only among the subjects of the control group who did not have any traumatic experience whatsoever (K_2), which we could have expected.

Our supposition is that a passive attitude and a passive role in coping with trauma effects are in positive correlation to the degree of the psychopathological response.

Table No. 19: The psychopathological features of subjects increased in terms of statistical significance in certain subgroups, obtained by answers to several questions (items) from LEAIQ
($E = E_1 + E_2$: E_1 – somatically traumatised at war, E_2 – somatically traumatised in peacetime)
($K = K_1 + K_2$: K_1 – mentally traumatised in peacetime, K_2 – no mental or somatic trauma whatsoever)

PSYCHO(PATHO)LOGICAL FEATURE OF THE TRAUMATISED INCREASED IN TERMS OF STATISTICAL SIGNIFICANCE	SUBGROUPS OF SUBJECTS IN WHICH CERTAIN FEATURE HAS BEEN SIGNIFICANTLY INCREASED	VARIANCE ANALYSIS VALUE(F)	STATISTICAL SIGNIFICANCE OF DIFFERENCES' LEVEL	SUBGROUPS OF SUBJECTS INCLUDED INTO STATISTICAL DATA PROCESSING
insomnia	E_1	$F_{1,121} = 9.36$	p<0.01	$E_1+E_2+K_1+K_2$
insomnia	K_1	$F_{2,112} = 3.51$	p<0.05	$E_1+E_2+K_1$
insomnia	E	$F_{1,173} = 12.50$	p<0.01	E+K
depressed mood	E_1+E_2	$F_{1,173} = 5.01$	p<0.05	$E_1+E_2+K_1+K_2$
somatisation	$E+K_1$	$F_{1,121} = 7.55$	p<0.01	$E_1+E_2+K_1+K_2$
somatisation	E	$F_{1,173} = 9.21$	p<0.01	E+K
anxiety	K_1	$F_{3,121} = 6.40$	p<0.01	$E_1+E_2+K_1+K_2$
anxiety	K_1	$F_{1,113} = 3.94$	p<0.05	$E+K_1$
general neuroticism	K_1+E_2	$F_{3,121} = 5.96$	p<0.01	$E_1+E_2+K_1+K_2$

c) Results obtained from the replies to one item related to a psychopathological feature

Below follows the analysis of certain narrower specific features of psychopathological response related to mental and somatic traumatic experience.

Statistical data processing obtained from the reply to only one question seems to confirm the overall results we obtained by using the previous methodology, superior in terms of objectivity and procedure reliability, but inferior in terms of qualitative analysis of psychopathological response of subjects, which we endeavoured to overcome by using this methodological procedure.

Table No. 20: Psychopathological features of subjects predominant in terms of statistical significance, obtained by replies to one question (item) only, taken from the questionnaires supplied by the subgroups
($E = E_1 + E_2$: E_1 – somatically traumatised at war, E_2 – somatically traumatised in peacetime, $K = K_1 + K_2$: K_1 – mentally traumatised in peacetime, K_2 – no mental or somatic trauma whatsoever)

DIAGNOSTIC CATEGORY OF PSYCHO-PATHOLOGICAL FEATURE	PSYCHO-PATHOLOGICAL FEATURE WHOSE STATISTICAL PRESENCE INSIGNIFICANTLY INCREASED	SUBGROUP IN WHICH CERTAIN FEATURE WAS SIGNIFICANTLY INCREASED	INSTRUMENT FROM WHICH THE ITEM RELATED TO THE FEATURE WAS TAKEN	χ^2 TEST VALUES	LEVEL OF STATISTICAL IMPORTANCE OF DIFFERENCES	SUBGROUPS OF SUBJ. INCLUDED INTO STATISTICAL DATA PROCESSING
	changes of mood	$E+K_1$	LEAIQ	$\chi^2 = 19.10$	p<0.01	$E_1+E_2+K_1+K_2$
	general capacity decrease	E_2+K_1	LEAIQ	$\chi^2 = 8.80$	p<0.05	$E_1+E_2+K_1+K_2$
	weakness	E_2+K_1	LEAIQ	$\chi^2 = 8.63$	p<0.05	$E_1+E_2+K_1+K_2$
Depressed mood	depressed mood	K_1	History	$\chi^2 = 71.05$	p<0.01	$E_1+E_2+K_1+K_2$
	depressed mood	E_1	History	$\chi^2 = 12.84$	p<0.05	$E_1+E_2+K_1$
	depressed mood	R	History	$\chi^2 = 29.22$	p<0.01	$E+K_1+K_2$
	depressed mood	R	History	$\chi^2 = 65.27$	p<0.01	$E+K_1+K_2$
	corporeal pains	E_2+K_1	LEAIQ	$\chi^2 = 10.39$	p<0.05	$E_1+E_2+K_1+K_2$
	headaches	$E_1+E_2+K_1$	LEAIQ	$\chi^2 = 10.12$	p<0.05	$E_1+E_2+K_1+K_2$
	vertigo	E_1	LEAIQ	$\chi^2 = 7.53$	p<0.05	$E_1+E_2+K_1$
Hysteria i.e. Conversion	vertigo	E_1+E_2	LEAIQ	$\chi^2 = 14.04$	p<0.01	$E_1+E_2+K_1+K_2$
	respiratory problems	E_1+E_2	LEAIQ	$\chi^2 = 13.38$	p<0.01	$E_1+E_2+K_1+K_2$
	disarrangement	E_1+K_1	History	$\chi^2 = 9.07$	p<0.01	$E_1+E_2+K_1+K_2$
	disarrangement	E_1+K_1	History	$\chi^2 = 13.68$	p<0.01	$E_1+E_2+K_2$
	disarrangement	E	History	$\chi^2 = 26.63$	p<0.01	E+K
	disarrangement	E	History	$\chi^2 = 29.05$	p<0.01	$E+K_1+K_2$
	nightmares	$E_1+E_2+K_1$	LEAIQ	$\chi^2 = 29.69$	p<0.01	$E_1+E_2+K_1+K_2$
	nightmares	K_1	LEAIQ	$\chi^2 = 9.01$	p<0.01	$E_1+E_2+K_1$
	tension	K_1	LEAIQ	$\chi^2 = 16.02$	p<0.01	$E_1+E_2+K_1+K_2$
	tension	K_1	LEAIQ	$\chi^2 = 9.66$	p<0.01	$E_1+E_2+K_1$
PTSD symptoms (unspecified neuroticism)	fear of situat. similar to trauma	K_1	LEAIQ	$\chi^2 = 11.55$	p<0.01	$E_1+E_2+K_1+K_2$
	fatigue	K_1	LEAIQ	$\chi^2 = 7.59$	p<0.05	$E_1+E_2+K_1$
	irritability	E_1+E_2	LEAIQ	$\chi^2 = 14.39$	p<0.01	$E_1+E_2+K_1$
	thoughts and feelings related to trauma	K_1	History	$\chi^2 = 13.93$	p<0.05	$E_1+E_2+K_1$
	thoughts and feelings related to trauma	K_1	History	$\chi^2 = 8.34$	p<0.05	E+K
	thoughts and feelings related to trauma	$E+K_1$	History	$\chi^2 = 52.01$	p<0.01	$E+K_1+K_2$

We took the questions consisting of specific items regarding the mental state assessment from the Late Effect of Accidental Injury Questionnaire (LEAIQ) and History (Past Experience).

We entered only the results related to the answers to certain (psychopathological) items, that is, questions which were, in terms of statistical significance, more manifested in the corresponding subgroup of subjects into Table No. 20. Therefore, the number of their citing in this table was an immediate quantitative measure of the importance of presence in the tested subgroup. We subsequently categorised the specific features, i.e. symptoms, into three larger diagnostic groups: depression, conversion or hysteria, and PTSD symptoms with certain symptoms of general neuroticism.

d) Summary of determined psychopathological features of traumatised patients

Table No. 21 presents the summary of statistically significantly increased psychopathological features of traumatised subjects. The number of appearances of certain psychopathological features is the result of calculating their presence in various combinations of the analysed subgroups. After the inspection of Table No. 21 presenting summarised results, the most common symptom obtained by statistical data processing using several items for one feature is psychogenic somatisation. It was confirmed as much as six times as significantly present in all three subgroups of traumatised subjects, but mostly among the traumatised at war. The symptom of insomnia follows, present in all neurotic disorders, and most frequently in depression. If this result is added to the one suggesting that the symptom of depression is significantly manifested in both subgroups of the somatically traumatised, the conclusion may be that depression as a symptom always follows psychogenic somatisation. The frequency of depressive reactions is therefore more noticeable, considering that some psychogenic symptoms may overlap with the symptoms that are the sequelae of the injury (in the experimental group). The symptom of anxiety takes the third place, ascertained as a significant one twice, and both times in the subgroup of mentally traumatised subjects.

General neuroticism, obtained by a different methodology application – from the answers to one question –, was distinguished only once in the somatically traumatised in the peacetime subgroup. Table No. 21 also shows that the individual symptom obtained from answers to one question only - »mental disarrangement« (appearing eight times) – appears 4 times in the somatically traumatised at war subgroup and twice in each subgroups of the somatically traumatised in peacetime and mentally traumatised in peacetime. »Depressive symptoms in a narrower sense« follow – appearing 6 times – 3 times in the subgroup with somatic war trauma subgroup, 2 times in the somatically traumatised in peacetime subgroup and once in the mentally traumatised in peacetime subgroup. Both »disarrangement« and »depressed mood«, in a phenomenological sense, proved in our research to be reliable qualitative psycho-pathological parameters of the severity of trauma, that is, differentiated variables whose significant presence also indirectly indicates the intensity, i.e. the destructive-ness of trauma. It is interesting that conversion symptoms – hysteria symptoms (de-termined by only one answer to a question) – were significantly manifested in the somatically traumatised at war subgroup (18 times), certain symptoms of depression in the subgroup of somatically traumatised in peacetime (5 times), and PTSD symp-toms in a narrower sense in the subgroup of mentally traumatised in peacetime (6 times).

The patients somatically traumatised in peacetime (E_2), being less neurotic in quantitative terms, are to a similar proportion less hysterical and less depressive in a qualitative sense, that is, less hysterical and depressive, when compared to the somati-cally traumatised at war.

The somatically traumatised in peacetime subgroup (K_1), in comparison to the pre-vious two subgroups, responded psychically in the most undefined manner. It is obvi-ous primarily from the fact that the most dominant presence of general neuroticism was observed in this subgroup, than from the (two times statistically significant) pres-ence of ›anxiety‹ in the subgroup, »the hazy source of a series of possible neurotic symptoms«, which, it should be pointed out, was present only in this subgroup. Only in this subgroup was ›tension‹ also registered (twice). The same is valid for the symp-toms of ›fear of the trauma-similar situation‹ significantly present only in this sub-group, while the symptom of ›thoughts and feelings related to trauma‹, similar to the symptoms of ›fear of the trauma-similar situation‹, appears in this subgroup three times more often than in the previous two subgroups of the traumatised in which it was registered only once.

It should be noted that concerning the typical symptoms of Posttraumatic Stress Disorder (nightmares, thoughts and feeling related to trauma, and the fear of the situa-tion similar to trauma), they were also most often registered in the mentally trauma-tised in peacetime subgroup as the most frequent ones (six times). In fact, the general score on PTSD scale was significantly present only once, as well as in the traumatised in peacetime subgroup, while in the traumatised at war subgroup it was present twice. The presence of general neurotic symptoms, and not of specific PTSD symptoms, may be responsible for this.

We should also mention the result that did not enter Table No. 21, suggesting a significantly increased total score on the Family Homogeneity Index in two combina-tions, namely, twice in the subgroup of individuals somatically traumatised at war (E_1), and once in the subgroup of subjects with no traumatic experience whatsoever (K_2). This result indicates, of course, *cum grano salis*, the assumption that on the one hand, the experience of intensity of family cohesiveness significantly increases in the families whose member has been severely injured (either somatically or mentally); on the other, the increased family cohesiveness itself is probably one of the perceptibility factors of such a traumatisation psychical effects, which was not the subject matter of this study. There is no doubt that the family gathers around its seriously injured member, especially if he/she is a younger person, as was the case with our subjects injured at war.

Table No. 21: The summary or features significantly more present in the responses of traumatised subjects

ORIGIN OF PSYCHOPATH. FEATURE (SUBGROUPS OF SUBJECTS)	PSYCHO-PATHOLO-GICAL FEATURES FROM THE INSTRU-MENT TOTAL SCORE	PSYCHOPATH OLOGICAL FEATURES FROM SEVE-RAL ITEMS OF THE INSTRUMENT	PSYCHOPATHOLOGICAL FEATURES FROM THE ANSWER TO ONE ITEM (QUESTION) OF CERTAIN INSTRUMENT	WIDER DIAGNOSTIC CATEGORY OF PSYCHOPATHOL. FEATURE
Somatically traumatised at war (E₁)	PTSD PTSD neuroticism	somatisation somatisation somatisation	disarrangement vertigo disarrangement vertigo disarrangement respiratory problems disarrangement headaches	hysteria i.e. conversion
		depressed mood insomnia insomnia	changes of mood depressed mood depressed mood depressed mood	depressed mood
			nightmares irritability thoughts and feelings related to trauma	unspecified neurosis
somatically traumatised in peacetime (E₂)	PTSD	somatisation somatisation	disarrangement vertigo disarrangement respiratory disorders physical pains headaches	hysteria i.e. conversion
		depressed mood insomnia	changes of mood general capacity decrease feeling of weakness depressed mood depressed mood	depressed mood
		general neuroticism	nightmares irritability thoughts and feelings related to trauma	unspecified neurosis
mentally traumatised in peacetime (K₁)	PTSD neuroticism	somatisation	disarrangement disarrangement corporeal pains headaches	hysteria i.e. conversion
		insomnia	changes of mood general capacity decrease weakness depressed mood	depressed mood
		anxiety anxiety general neuroticism	nightmares fear of situation similar to trauma nightmares thoughts and feelings rel. to trauma tension thoughts and feelings rel. to trauma tension thoughts and feelings rel. to trauma fatigue	unspecified neurosis

115

2.4. Specific traumatisation circumstances and psychopathological response to trauma

We endeavoured to find out what, in addition to somatic or mental trauma itself, could have influenced the psychopathological response of our subjects. In the literature related to this issue, several factors are mentioned which could, each in its own way, have had an impact on the psychopathological response of the subjects, and we wanted to verify their possible significance for the studied phenomenon.

An unavoidable factor of psychological response to trauma, good preparedness for trauma (according to our results, significantly more present in as much as four different combinations of statistical data processing related to subjects with traumatic experience, either at war or in peacetime), almost totally annuls the impact of trauma suddenness, that is, unpreparedness for the injury, on the psychopathology of responding to traumas. Frequency of good preparedness for trauma (four times) in the somatically traumatised at war subgroup is understandable, considering the state of war, but it is present (two times) also among the somatically traumatised in peacetime, and even once in the mentally traumatised in peacetime subgroup (see Table No. 22).

Unpreparedness for trauma, on the other hand, differentiates certain types of psychopathological responses. Among the subjects who showed a mild paranoid feature (based upon the answer to only one question) there were significantly more ($F_{1.68} = 4.70$; $p < 0.05$) of those who were not warned of the forthcoming calamity. We also found that among the depressive subjects (based upon 5 items from the Late Effect of Accidental Injury Questionnaire – LEAIQ) there were, in terms of statistical significance, more of those ($F_{1.68} = 5.89$; $p < 0.05$) who experienced trauma without being prepared for it.

In short, unpreparedness for trauma in our case predisposed towards a partially paranoid, and very clearly depressive, way of responding in the subjects with physical traumas.

The fact that somatic trauma is more intensive in comparison to mental trauma (control subgroup) was confirmed in as many as four different combinations of statistical data processing. In both experimental subgroups (with somatic trauma), the experience of high-intensity trauma was found to be predominant (most probably, primarily the painfulness and inability to walk with all sequelae) in comparison to other subgroups of subjects.

Most probably, the experience of trauma intensity also has elements of the life threat experience (the thought of dying in the accident), which was also significantly increased in subjects of both subgroups of somatically traumatised individuals – four times in the subgroup of subjects with war traumas and three times in the subgroup of subjects with somatic traumas during peacetime (see Table No. 22).

116

Table No. 22: Features of trauma conditions predominant in terms of statistical significance
(obtained from the History – past experience)
(E = E₁ + E₂ : E₁ – somatic war trauma, E₂ – somatic peacetime trauma)
(K = K₁ + K₂ : K₁ – mental peacetime trauma, K₂ – no mental or somatic trauma whatsoever)

PSYCHO(PATHO)LOGICAL FEATURE WITH STATISTICALLY SIGNIFICANT PRESENCE INCREASE	SUBGROUP OF SUBJECTS WITH SIGNIFICANT INCREASE OF THE PRESENCE OF CERTAIN FEATURE	χ^2- TEST VALUE	"P"-VALUE	SUBGROUPS AMONG WHICH STATISTICAL PROCESSING OF DIFFERENCES IN THE PRESENCE OF PSYCHO(PATHO)LOGICAL FEATURE WAS CONDUCTED
well prepared for trauma	E_1	$\chi^2 = 29.80$	p<0,01	$E_1+E_2+K_1$
	E_1	$\chi^2 = 33.61$	p<0,01	$E_1+E_2+K_1+K_2$
	E	$\chi^2 = 9.03$	p<0,05	E+K
	$E+K_2$	$\chi^2 = 14.32$	p<0,05	$E+K_1+K_2$
high intensity of traumatic experience	$E_1 + E_2$	$\chi^2 = 169.47$	p<0,01	$E_1+E_2+K_1+K_2$
	$E_1 + E_2$	$\chi^2 = 41.91$	p<0,01	$E_1+E_2+K_1$
	E	$\chi^2 = 39.27$	p<0,01	E+K
	$E_1 + E_2$	$\chi^2 = 41.37$	p<0,01	$E+K_1+K_2$
thought of dying in trauma	E_1	$\chi^2 = 33.61$	p<0,01	$E_1+E_2+K_1+K_2$
	E	$\chi^2 = 6.29$	p<0,05	E+K
	E_1	$\chi^2 = 17.83$	p<0,01	E_1+E_2
	$E_1 + E_2$	$\chi^2 = 11.18$	p<0,01	$E+K_1+K_2$
a close person died in the same accident	E_1	$\chi^2 = 45.81$	p<0,01	$E_1+E_2+K_1+K_2$
	E_1	$\chi^2 = 12.10$	p<0,01	E_1+E_2
loss of home in the same trauma	E_1	$\chi^2 = 11.72$	p<0,01	$E_1+E_2+K_1$
	E_1	$\chi^2 = 23.66$	p<0,01	$E_1+E_2+K_1+K_2$
	E	$\chi^2 = 7.00$	p<0,01	E+K

The experienced traumatisation of the somatically injured at war, as a leading one, was also confirmed through the result according to which a close person had died in the same accident (twice only in that subgroup), as well as the findings that these subjects had lost their homes in the same trauma (in as much as three repeated calculations).

All in all, through applying this methodological procedure, the increased proneness to psychopathological response was registered to be predominant among the somatically traumatised at war, then, among the somatically traumatised in peacetime. These findings can be explained by previously obtained results, that is, the experience of a life threat during traumatisation, the fact that a close person had died in the same accident, and the loss of a home in the same trauma. The suddenness of trauma plays no special role in these circumstances. In other words, what makes the experience of trauma intensity are the factors which are related not only to physical injury as such but to the circumstances resulting from the accompanying aspects of traumatisation (co-morbidity factors).

2.5 Coping with trauma effects

The psychopathological effects of traumatisation can be also investigated in the light of the ways subjects cope with trauma, immediately following the traumatisation, or in the long run.

It is interesting that on average, somatically traumatised patients were rather ambivalent in their attitude toward coping with trauma effects. In terms of statistical significance (see Table No. 22) and in comparison to the control subgroup with subjects mentally traumatised in peacetime, they more often adopted both an active and a passive attitude in coping with trauma effects. This can be explained by their difficult state, which makes them passive, and at the same time, by the series of frustrations and sufferings which makes the injured take an active attitude in coping with them. It cannot be excluded that the instrument used was not differentiating enough for analysing the issue in our population.

The above mentioned ambivalence was emphasised among the subjects with somatic war trauma (E_1) who believed the others were responsible for their calamity, but at the same time felt significantly better in the company of other people. It is very probable that they took the former ›others‹ to be public figures or possibly the members of other ethnic groups or even members of NATO forces (bearing in mind the circumstances in which Bosnian Serbs were being injured), while the latter ›others‹ were most probably close relatives and friends or health care workers taking care of them. This conclusion is supported by the findings that their feeling better in the company of others was confirmed as much as three times in both the subgroup of those somatically traumatised at war and the subgroup of those injured at peacetime.

Among the subjects with an active attitude in coping with the effects of somatic injury, the feature of ›defended one's home and property‹ was significantly more present ($F_{1.51} = 6.99$; p<0.05), which suggests that an active attitude in coping with the effects of trauma was triggered by all events which occurred during traumatisation, which made the injured cope with trauma effects (the war during which the subjects were injured defending their homes).

It is very interesting that a relatively rapid onset of acute shock (1-3 days following the injury in comparison to that of 4 or 7 days of coping with the shock after trauma) produces a significantly higher ($F_{3.38} = 5.52$; p<0.05) presence of paranoid experience in our subjects.

It was also concluded that the subjects who were coping with their accidents longer (more than 12 hours in comparison to those who needed less than 12 hours to cope with it) gave significantly higher estimates of the homogeneity of their immediate families. It may be assumed that the above-mentioned high degree of family cohesion was indeed one of the factors of such a long period of coping with accident effects. However, the assumption that family cohesion strengthens when the family

118

system is being tested is supported by the result at which we arrived – among the subjects with a high degree of family homogeneity, those whose close relatives died in the same accident were in a significant majority ($F_{1.68} = 4.46$; $p < 0.05$).

Table No. 23: The features of subjects more present in terms of statistical significance and related
to coping with traumatisation
(E = E$_1$ + E$_2$: E$_1$ – somatically traumatised at war, E$_2$ – somatically traumatised in peacetime)
(K = K$_1$ + K$_2$: K$_1$ – mentally traumatised in peacetime, K$_2$ – no mental or somatic trauma whatsoever)

SUBGROUP OF SUBJECTS IN WHICH THE TESTED FEATURE IS SIGNIFICANTLY MORE PRESENT	COPING WITH TRAUMATISATION FEATURE	INSTRUMENT FROM WHICH THE COPING WITH TRAUMA FEATURE WAS TAKEN	χ^2 - TEST VALUE OR F FROM THE VARIANCE ANALYSIS	"P"- VALUE	SUBGROUPS IN WHICH STATISTICAL PROCESSING WAS CARRIED OUT
E	active attitude in coping with trauma	5 items of Impact on Events Scale	$F_{1.173} = 26.13$	p<0,01	E+K
E	passive attitude in coping with trauma	10 items of Impact on Events Scale	$F_{1.173} = 31.76$	p<0,01	E+K
E$_1$	has the objections to treatment	Late Effects of Accidental Injury Questionnaire	$\chi^2 = 9.89$	p<0,05	E$_1$+E$_2$
E$_1$	believes the others are responsible for his trauma	Late Effects of Accidental Injury Questionnaire	$\chi^2 = 6.09$	p<0,05	E$_1$+E$_2$
E$_1$+ E$_2$	feels better in company of other people	History	$\chi^2 = 15.51$	p<0,05	E$_1$+E$_2$+K$_1$
E	feels better in company of other people	History	$\chi^2 = 20.35$	p<0,01	E+K
E	feels better in company of other people	History	$\chi^2 = 20.90$	p<0,01	E+K$_1$+K$_2$

2.6 Summary of our research results in comparison to similar research

We shall attempt to make a comparison between the main results of our research with similar research carried out by other authors, mainly of recent date, which is justified by several reasons.

A part of socio-demographic variables in our research (religious affiliation and profession) did not significantly shape the psychopathological response of either somatically or mentally traumatised subjects. However, Wilcox, Briones, Suess (1991) found more of the so-called severe psychic disorders (audio hallucinations and the like) among US veterans of Hispanic origins.

Regarding the impact of gender – the first socio-demographic variable – on the psychopathological response of subjects to trauma, women were identified to suffer from insomnia, depression and anxiety significantly more often. The finding is most probably related to findings according to which, women were, at the same time, more extrovert. (On the other hand, there were very few of them among the subjects somatically traumatised at war, the subgroup in which psychopathological response was the most obvious.) The reason for their more severe psychopathological response to somatic trauma might be their physical constitution, i.e. their hormonal status, which was observed by many authors to be associated with their neurotic response (Opalić, 1990).

Findings similar to ours were provided by Potts (1994), whose study investigated Japanese civilians interned in U.S. camps during World War II (especially for longer periods of time). Female subjects included in the study manifested an increased proneness towards the response to stress. Peltzer (1995), upon referencing it with various studies related to the issue, concluded that women were more sensitive to stress than men, especially in the time immediately following trauma. It is hard not to get the same impression as some psychologists, psychotherapists and sociologists (Papić 1992), stating that women, in all circumstances (and following a trauma as well), »use« body language as some kind of communication, thus continuing ›dialogue‹ with their environment when they cannot do it by means of conventional language. A result similar to ours was also arrived at by Feinstein, Dolan (1991) who, studying PTSD in people after somatic injury (using, among others instruments, GHQ-60), concluded that not a single socio-demographic variable differentiated proneness towards PTSD, except that in women there were significantly more life events.

Drozdek (1997) found that in a population very much like our Serb population – Bosniaks from Bosnia and Herzegovina (refugees in the Netherlands) –, socio-demographic variables, including gender and age, had no significant impact on the psychopathological status. Similarly, Jovanović et al. (1997) also did not find that in a population almost identical to ours, gender, profession, the household type or financial status of subjects differentiated GAF (Global Assessment of Functions Scale) scores among the patients exposed to a series of stress-inducing situations, including injuries. (In the aforesaid study, a significantly lower GAF score was obtained by refugees and unmarried, widowed and divorced subjects). Amundsen G. et al. (1998) also validated that neither gender nor age or marital status affected the tendency to Posttraumatic Stress Disorder among 139 subjects with work-related injuries.

Concerning the socio-demographic variable of marital status, it should be repeated that our research confirmed that ›single‹ subjects (non-married ones) were significantly more neurotic (according to Eysenck's Brief Personality Inventory).

Our research also verified some of already recognised results of the investigations similar to ours (Peltzer, 1995; Kaličanin, Bjelogrlić, Petković, 1992; WHO 1992), reporting that the highest-risk groups exposed to trauma are children and the elderly. Elderly subjects injured at war were found to be significantly more suicidal, depressive and paranoid; in other words, they were on average more destabilised psychologically than younger subjects. Significantly impaired cognitive functions (concentra-

120

tion and memory disorders) were reported among elderly subjects as well. Elderly subjects somatically traumatised during peacetime were also more neurotic in a general sense (PTSD scale and Brief Eysenck's Personality Inventory) than younger subjects in all studied subgroups. Similar findings, showing that the elderly manifested several symptoms as responses to stress, were obtained in a study by Weine S. et al. (1998) investigating a similar population – Muslim refugees from Bosnia in the USA –, as well as in a study by Potts (1994) of the Japanese internees in U.S. camps during World War II.

The increased psychological vulnerability of the elderly was, in our research, certainly associated with their other features as well. This primarily refers to a decreased family cohesiveness among the elderly subjects. Similar results were obtained by Orr, Aronson (1990), whose study revealed a significantly decreased evaluation of family and social support among elderly traumatised patients in orthopaedic rehabilitation.

However, the overall impression is that there are more studies in literature (Atanasijević, 1996: Hume, Summerfield 1994; Solomon, Mikulincer 1987) showing that the psychopathological responses to stress and physical trauma, respectively, are not differentiated by the subjects' age.

Regarding education, it was confirmed in our study that the subjects with a lower level of education (elementary school only), in comparison to those with a higher level of education (secondary or higher education), suffered significantly more from psychogenic somatic disorders in all three subgroups of the traumatised. It is a fact confirmed by several researches (Opalić 1990) that people with lower education tended more towards conversion as a way of processing their fear and tension arising from stressful situations. It is interesting that the subjects with elementary and secondary education took a more passive attitude in coping with trauma effects than those with a higher education, which is probably also related to some other factors of psychopathological response.

Another study (Atanasijević 1996) reported that those subjects with a higher education level in a similar situation (female refugees in Yugoslavia), in comparison to those with a lower education level, more often used mature mechanisms of resolving the effects (mechanisms directed towards problems, family or work) than less mature ones, the so-called palliative mechanisms (turning for support, avoiding to think about it, etc.), which confirmed what the researches had suspected – the cognitive preparedness for trauma plays a positive role in the psychological response to accidents.

However, education did not differentiate the psychopathological response of subjects in research by Solomon, Mikulincer (1987), as was also found in a study by Jovanovic et al. (1996) performed on a very similar population.

One of the key findings we arrived at is an increased tendency towards the development of PTSD in all three subgroups of traumatised subjects. The next result reveals that most subjects with PTSD were in the subgroup with somatic war trauma, although the subgroup was comprised of mainly younger subjects. We discovered the reason for the increased proneness towards PTSD development among these subjects in some other results related to this subgroup – there were statistically significantly more subjects with the experience of life threat, as well as subjects with a close person's death in the same accident. Even the increased family cohesiveness determined in this subgroup did not protect these subjects from a more distinct psychopathological response.

Group cohesiveness, as shown by some other research, for example, with Vietnam war veterans (Fontana, Rosenheck, Horvath 1997) or with German soldiers deployed to UN peace-keeping missions in Bosnia during the civil war in former Yugoslavia (Schunk, Shade, Schüffel 1998), is a reliable preventive factor of PTSD development. However, another study showed completely different results: The study by Jovanović A. (1997) of 160 subjects – Serbs with a similar, but more traumatic experience (being tortured in Bosnian and Croatian prisons) and with PTSD diagnosis – found that they achieved a significantly lower score on the Family Homogeneity Index (FHI), the instrument we also used. It appeared that somatic trauma, contrary to mental trauma, affected family relations to a lesser degree, and, according to the results of our study, it led to family homogenisation. This conclusion was confirmed by our study results, indicating that the subjects who coped with the accident for a longer period of time (over 12 hours), in comparison to those coping with the accident less than 12 hours, estimated the cohesiveness of their families to be significantly higher.

The GHQ-60 – General Health Questionnaire – in its total score did not differentiate various subgroups of subjects, although there are studies (Hume, Summerfield 1994) according to which the score achieved on this instrument correlated positively with the psychopathological response of subjects with somatic war trauma.

As for the quality, that is, the clinical presentation of psychopathological response, we determined that anxiety dominated in the subgroup of subjects with mental trauma experienced during peacetime (control subgroup with mental traumatic experience). Insomnia and psychogenic somatisation were predominant in all three subgroups of traumatised subjects, while a depressed mood was most present in both subgroups of somatically traumatised subjects.

When considering, conditionally speaking, the quantity of psychopathological responses (i.e., the number of statistically significant psychopathological features of neuroticism whose presence is determined, as well as total scores achieved by the instrument), the subjects with somatic war trauma take the first place. The second are, relatively unexpectedly, the subjects from the subgroup of those mentally traumatised during peacetime, and the third are the subjects with somatic trauma during peacetime. All in all, subjects with somatic war trauma responded to it in the most intensive way in the quantitative sense, and in the most differentiated way in the qualitative sense (conversion and depression).

122

The subjects with somatic trauma during peacetime are, quantitatively speaking, less neurotic, but qualitatively speaking, less differentiated. The features of general neuroticism dominate in this subgroup, followed by somatogenic symptoms.

The subgroup of those mentally traumatised during peacetime (most probably without the experience of physical trauma) responded in an extremely unspecific manner, psychopathologically speaking. In addition, the symptoms of Posttraumatic Stress Disorder appear in this group most often, among the signs of general neuroticism.

Regarding narrower clinical features of neuroticism, fully differentiated states of mental disorders of somatically or mentally traumatised subjects from Serbia, the symptom of psychogenic somatisation was the most prevailing one. Such findings may probably be related to the mentality of South Eastern European regions (Greeks, Italians, Turks, etc.), where the frequency of this type of neurotic disorders was noticed to be extremely high (Opalić 1990). A study of the Posttraumatic Stress Disorder in 804 Israeli soldiers by Solomon, Mikulincer (1987) also reported the prevalence of somatisation complaints (while the exposure to stress essentially affected somatisation duration).

The insomnia, relatively unspecific, but most commonly conditioned with depression, was in the second place, while depression in its narrow sense took the third. The anxiety was only in the fourth place. This result, i.e. high depression rate, corresponds to the observations of some other authors, who have recently found that Posttraumatic Stress Disorder in subjects from various environments are manifested in an anxiety-depressive clinical state. Namely, these studies were related to the investigation of civil trauma victims' responses (Davis, Breslau 1994) and political prisoners in the former GDR's responses (Denis, Eslam, Priebe 1997).

The manifestation of conversion symptoms as the most common phenomena was verified in our study through the analysis of answers to one question of certain instruments only, and again as the most prominent in the subgroup of subjects with somatic war trauma. Among these symptoms, the experience of distress was at the forefront (with the elements of psychogenic dissociation), and the following were: vertigo, headache, respiratory disorders and physical pains. The symptoms of general neuroticism were the subsequent ones (such as they were or under other names like irritability, tension, fatigue). In these symptoms we also included those typical of Posttraumatic Stress Disorder, which were the most frequent in the subgroup of those mentally traumatised in peacetime anyway (fear from the situation similar to trauma, thoughts and feelings related to trauma, and especially nightmares). We particularly emphasised the last symptom since it is well-known (Schreuder 1995) that there is a high correlation between nightmares and the intensity of war experience.

Amputation itself, most often carried out after a work-related injury, did not differentiate a specific kind of psychopathological response, which could be expected.

Most probably, it is a result of the fact that the overall number of amputees was low and the fact that they were still not in the situation to express potential psychic changes, which usually occur later, as determined by Vujko, Kuzmanović, Božović (1994) in amputees from a similar population. Among Serb and Yugoslav amputees, Jovanovic A. et al. (1997) have determined increased values on the Impact of Events Scale and Hopelessness Scale, that is, reactive psychiatric disorders (PTSD, prolonged depressive response, adjustment disorders) in around 20% of refugees that are amputees. These results confirm that somatic trauma related to a difficult psychosocial situation (refugee status) results in a high percentage of psychical disorders, which was indirectly confirmed by our study (somatic trauma associated with the loss of home or a close person).

The World Health Organisation Declaration (WHO 1992) and the results of some research on the Serb population (Kaličanin, Bjelogrlić, Petković 1992) suggest that population groups with the highest risk – in terms of possible psychopathological responses – were former psychiatric patients, members of their families, front-line combatants and refugees. This was indirectly confirmed by our study. Prior to their being injured, only half of the control group subjects – those without any trauma whatsoever – did not have any problems with nerves, who in all variants of calculations, proved to be the most psychologically stable. Moreover, we could raise the question (especially in comparing this subgroup with the subgroup of peacetime subjects who experienced some trauma in their lifetime) to what an extent so-called problems with nerves take part in creating a so-called accident-prone person. Some research (Whitlock, Stoll, Rekhdahl 1977) has confirmed that the persons who had been injured in a traffic accident had had significantly more stress-inducing life events prior to the accident. Other research (Macklin et al. 1998; Jin et al. 1991) has found that subjects with lower intelligence had a tendency to develop PTSD, that is, they were traffic-accident prone persons.

The factor of surprise, i.e. unpreparedness for trauma, did not play a special role in the psychopathological response of our subjects, maybe because at the same time we determined good preparedness for trauma in all three subgroups of somatically or mentally traumatised subjects. We only determined that the subjects who had not had time to prepare for the accident significantly more often responded in a more depressive and partially more (only at the level of statistical trend) paranoid manner. Very similar results on a similar population (Vietnam soldiers) were arrived at by Watson et al. (1993).

Although some research (Wyshak 1994) showed that the number of information on the conditions of traumatisation were in reverse proportion to the number of accompanying psychological symptoms of trauma, we managed to get a lot of relevant information on conditions of traumatisation in all subgroups of our sample. Thus, the experience of traumatic intensity in our study was confirmed to be significantly more present in both subgroups of subjects with physical trauma, although it was most present in the subgroup of subjects who had been somatically injured at war. It is almost certain that the evaluation of injury intensity is closely related to three other features of traumatisation, one partially subjective (thoughts of being killed in the accident) and other so-called objective indicators of accident severity, with the fact that the subject had lost a close person or home in the same accident. It suggests as a conclusion that very difficult war conditions significantly influence possible psycho-pathological response of the wounded. However, it can be assumed that somatic injury itself does not play as significant a role as other accompanying traumatic phenomena, or it is probably the accumulation of all effects that matters. The importance of co-morbidity for psychopathological response of those somatically traumatised is also indicated by the result of a similar research (Delimar et al. 1998) on Croatian soldiers in the same civil war in former Yugoslavia, revealing that the subjects with less severe somatic injuries developed more symptoms of Posttraumatic Stress Disorder. If we may comment, the issue in the latter case was maybe the secondary or tertiary benefit from the injury, which was verified in Yugoslav society in the 1950s by the so-called partisan neurosis (hysterical attacks of former soldiers in the form of combat assault, who unconsciously elicit more merits from the state and their surroundings for their deeds following World War II - Klajn 1995). This phenomenon was insignificantly present among Serb soldiers wounded during the civil war in former Yugoslavia – the subjects of our study being largely ignored by the public and state institutions in Ser-bia (and treated mostly like ordinary invalids, and in no way like war heroes), as was not the case with partisans and as appears not to be the case with »victorious« soldiers of the independent state of Croatia.

Anyhow, the common result of such studies is that the severity of somatic impair-ments is followed by the intensity of the psychopathological symptoms independently of other factors. It was verified by Winter (1996), whose sample comprised of subjects injured in traffic accidents, then, in studies of Vietnam soldiers by Buydens-Branchey et al. (1990) and Watson et al. (1993), as well as in a study of former Nicaraguan soldiers by Hume, Summerfield (1994).

As to coping with trauma effects, we determined that the most seriously injured subjects, i.e. those with somatic war traumas, did have an extremely ambivalent atti-tude towards coping with trauma effects. They showed a significantly active and at the same time significantly passive attitude towards this issue. It is well known from studies (Winter H., 1996) investigating traffic accidents that those subjects who ex-perienced a life threat in accidents later manifested a passive attitude in coping with accident effects. Their state of being frightened, and their depressive mood, that is, the negative picture they have of themselves immediately following the accident, indicate a worse prognosis of psychological recovery.

Those injured at war significantly more often believed others were responsible for their accident, which is understandable considering that during the war, individuals usually do not decide on moments crucial to their injury or their losses. On the contrary, our subjects with physical traumas in both subgroups felt better in the company of other people, which leads to the conclusion that their need for interpersonal relations was less thwarted, a need (Vlajković 1997) which is, along with alleviating unpleasant feelings and the level of preserved self-respect, a key criterion in the evaluation of the efficacy of coping with trauma effects.

There is no doubt that in coping with stress-inducing trauma effects, other factors play a certain role, the factors of accident we did not analyse directly, such as stress vagueness, the fact that those exposed to stress are overburdened with tasks, and, the existential significance of trauma- stricken areas of life (Berger 1997).

Ending this paper, we could conclude – paraphrasing a well-known research in literature carried out by Raphael, Lundin, Weisaeth (1989) – that we analysed in the Serb (mainly Belgrade) population of the 90's a majority of the main aspects of psychopathological response to somatic traumatisation. Certain specific features of the response were determined, those related to clinical state, co-morbidity, as well as the psychological state of subjects related to certain specific traumatisation conditions and coping with it.

Resume

The introduction section first offers the main reasons for psychopathological phenomena accompanying somatic injuries. The next, key section of the paper presents the research objectives, and then presents the sample consisting of 70 patients hospitalised at the Orthopaedic Hospital of the University Clinical Centre, Belgrade, due to severe physical injury (26 war veterans from Bosnia and Herzegovina and 44 Belgrade residents injured at work, during leisure or in traffic accidents), who comprised the experimental group. The control group comprised 105 subjects, out of whom 45 had mental trauma and 60 had no trauma experience whatsoever.

The subjects were tested with the following instruments: Impact of Events Scale, PTSD-10 Scale, Family Homogeneity Index (FHI), Brief Eysenck's Personality Inventory, Late Effects of Accidental Injury Questionnaire (LEAIQ), General Health Questionnaire (GH-60), General Questionnaire for Accidents, and two instruments involving the subjects' history and their way of responding to accident effects. In the statistical data processing, Analysis of Variance (ANOVA), Pearson's χ^2 test, discrimination analysis and calculation of linear correlation were used.

As to the psycho-pathological characteristics of the somatically injured subjects, it was determined that subjects over 30 years of age, as well as married subjects, re-

sponded considerably more frequently with cognitive neurotic symptoms (impaired memory and weak concentration). Unmarried subjects more often responded with PTSD symptoms, while single ones, after somatic trauma, responded more neurotically according to Eysenck's Personality Inventory.

The highest degree of family cohesion was recorded in the group of subjects with somatic war trauma. Subjects with a lower degree of education responded with conversion neurotic disorders significantly more often.

The highest degree of neuroticism and proneness to PTSD reactions, as well as an array of neurotic responses, were identified in the group of subjects with somatic war trauma, then, among subjects generally traumatised in peacetime, and finally, in the group with somatic peacetime traumas. This result was supported with a statistically significant relatedness of somatic war traumas with the experience of life threat, loss of a close family member or a home in the same trauma.

In a qualitative sense, the symptoms of neurotic somatisation (within whom the feeling of being distracted, light-headedness, headache) take the lead, followed by insomnia and depressive symptoms and, finally, anxiety. Subjects from the group with somatic war trauma responded mostly with conversive symptoms, those from the group with peacetime somatic trauma with conversive and depressive neurotic disturbances, and those from the group of subjects generally traumatised in peacetime mostly with PTSD symptoms.

»Nerve problems« before trauma were found significantly most frequently in the subjects from the group of those somatically traumatised in peacetime.

Subjects who had not been prepared for the accident responded with a higher degree of depression and paranoia.

The most severely injured subjects in our research (those injured at war) showed an ambivalent attitude toward coping with trauma effects, as well as a tendency to consider others, not themselves, responsible for their injury.

It was determined that the external circumstances of injury (traffic accident, work and war) did not differentiate any of the psychological or psychopathological types of responses analysed in the research. It was determined that a difficult surgical procedure performed under general anaesthesia positively correlates with PTSD symptoms. It was also confirmed that the immobility of a patient significantly correlates with his/her general neuroticism and insomnia.

IV

Human Figure Test in the Research of Psycho(patho)logical State of Refugees and Somatically Traumatised Subjects

Introduction

The research of trauma effects is, in most cases, based on the results obtained by using psychometric instruments (questionnaires, interviews) or on the results that originate from purely clinical trials (auto- and hetero-anamnesis, that is, life histories of subjects). As of the former approach, in our previous research (Opalić, Lešić 2001), we did the same in the investigation of somatically and mentally traumatised persons.

Using the Machover Test or Human Figure Test in this study should enable a »softening« and qualitative enrichment of the results obtained by purely quantitative methods of examining the mental state of subjects via psychometric instruments. This heuristic area to which the method is applied in the investigation of the mental state of those afflicted is, first of all, an involuntary motor or grapho-motor expression of mental status, difficult to access by means of other, verbal or symbolic, research instruments, which are, as psychoanalysts point out with good reason, under a stricter censorship of the conscious contents of mind and socially expected responses.

Research Goals and Hypotheses

The general goal of this research is to determine similarities and differences in potential psychopathological reactions to trauma in general, that is, to distress caused by a refugee situation on one side, and somatic injury of the subject on the other. The Human Figure Test applied in this research provides a specific, graphically-projected point of view in attaining the general goal.

Moreover, specific goals, as well as hypotheses of the research, are related to the general goal. These are as follows:

1. To determine the specific quality of the impact of the refugee situation and somatic trauma on graphic, i.e. projective, aspects of the human figure drawing, in the first place, the drawing of oneself. Namely, we expect a higher degree of presence of general psychopathological features in the drawings of somatically traumatised persons and refugees in comparison to non-traumatised subjects.

2. To confirm possible differences in the results obtained by the application of the Machover Test in refugees and somatically injured persons, in a narrower diagnostic sense. We expect, in qualitative and quantitative terms, more clearly defined psychiatric disorders in the refugee population, while of somatically injured persons, we expect more signs of mental disorders related to the body scheme experience.

3. To verify the impact of socio-demographic features of subjects (sex, age, marital status, family status) on possible differences in the features of human

131

figure drawing concerning the psychopathologic state of the subject. We presume, specifically, that female and elderly subjects, as well as less educated and single ones, react to the human figure drawing with more general signs of mental disorder than their socio-demographic opponents.

4. To determine the impact somatic trauma experience has on the features of graphical assessment of the body, i.e. on the body scheme (body image = image of the experience of one's own body) of somatically injured subjects. We presume, in particular, more obvious and more significant traces of the graphical presence of mental disintegration in those parts of the human figure drawing which express, directly or in a symbolic manner, the injured part of the body, and possibly the body of somatically traumatised subjects as a whole.

Research Method

a) Research Instrument – Machover Test

Although in a certain way archaic, the Machover Test (1965) or Human Figure Test, the main instrument of this research, was used for the evaluation of certain, more difficult to perceive aspects of the mental state of subjects, primarily, involuntary layers of mental life which concern graphic, i.e. expressive (spontaneous) or authentic behaviour of subjects in general. Besides, as pointed out by Berger (1984), the instrument is relatively simple, does not frustrate subjects and is easy to fill in, although, as further maintained by this author, it may also express current needs or interpersonal conflicts of the subjects.

In the evaluation of human figure drawing, one should take into account the features such as size, symmetry, thickness and line continuity etc., which are mainly of graphical nature. In addition, features concerning the so-called oddness of the drawing, such as the absence of body parts, erasing, improving, shading or bizarreness of the human figure drawing are also to be evaluated. Considering that this instrument, unlike the majority of others, expresses the entirety of the body scheme experience of subjects, it is suitable for the determination of the features of body limits of one's own ego (Uzelac 1973). When the latter aspect of this instrument is concerned, it is, psychoanalytically speaking, probably a matter of changing one's direction in investing energy of one's libido towards the injured or diseased part of the body, considering that this process is closely related to the maintenance of total mental integrity of the subject. Psychoanalysts (Erić 2000, p. 102) state, supported by valid arguments, that the »graphical expression of mentally ill persons poses an attempt aimed at restitution and ending further ego regression«. Therefore, this instrument also indirectly examines the degree of psychosexual development of the subjects, also insisted on by its author.

In accordance with our theoretical orientation (Opalić 1998, 1999), we shall rely on psychoanalysis in interpreting the Machover Test results, »elaborating« it, when necessary according to our estimation, with existential theoretical interpretations. Our intention will primarily concern evaluations of certain details of human figure drawing, as well as the impression of the overall personality structure. When the former evaluation aspects are concerned, we cannot but mention certain existential-analytical interpretations of the human figure drawing which offer themselves at the first glance. Drawing a head, for instance, is the basis for the evaluation of intellectual aspirations and rational control of subjects, drawing eyes constitutes the basis for the evaluation of the subject's attitude towards the world, especially of his way of experiencing social environment, while drawing ears is the basis of registering the experience of the environment towards the subject, etc.

Certain researchers using this instrument (Pražić 1971) claim that formal graphical solutions in the drawing are in direct proportional correlation with the affective stability of the patient. »An emotionally disturbed personality has a relatively incorrect perception of the world, since that observation has been ›invested‹ with his/her own experiences, feelings, needs and attitudes«, Lj. Stojanović wrote (1973, p. 5). Stojanović further maintatins that there is an essential feature correspondence in the drawings made by the same subject in a time series. This characteristic provides to the Machover Test, beside other things, the much-needed reliability.

In the past, this test was practically the constituent part of almost all psychological batteries of clinical trials (Todorović 1973). The reason why this is no longer the case may be due to its shortcomings (relative subjectivity conditioned by the mental dynamics of the researcher), its descriptiveness, i.e. difficulties in quantifying graphical results of the examination, and, finally, the relative dependence of the research results on other subject data. However, the Human Figure Test has for the last twenty years been successfully applied both in this country (Marković 1973; Todorović 1973; Uzelac 1973; Kron 1993; Jovanović, Đurović 2002), and worldwide (Schilder 1950). The researchers use it, first of all, to determine nuances in the evaluation of deeper layers of the mental state of subjects, among which children constituted the majority.

The Machover Test concerns, no doubt, the experience of one's own personality as a whole, even in the situation when the subject has to respond to universal requirements, such as: »Draw a human figure.« We gave our subjects two explicit requirements – »Draw a male human figure« and »Draw a female human figure«, each on a separate piece of A4 paper –, while at the same time restraining ourselves from giving any instructions on the manner of performing the test. At the end, we evaluated only the drawing of the figure concerning the subject's gender.

In this research, we decided to take into consideration those graphical contents of this test that are the result of selection from several sources – first of all, the selection from the elements by this method's original author, that is, elements found in her study »Personality Projection in the Drawing of the Human Figure« (Machover 1965), and then from the elements of subsequent adaptations of the same instrument by other authors (Berger 1984; Kron 1993). More precisely, we sorted out 16 features of the drawings of human figures which reveal potentially changed mental status of subjects: atypical form of the drawing, bizarre or unusual contents of the drawing, discontinuity or interruption of the figure line, thickened line, outstanding disproportion of certain parts of the figure, decentring of the drawing in relation to the paper (drawing very close to the paper edge), figure drawn in imbalance, emphasised figure asymmetry, unclear medium line of human figure, extremities pressed close to the body (legs and arms), absence of an arm or a leg, shading of drawing, extremely large human figure, figure without hands or without feet, and finally, fingers or toes drawn. At the same time, we should emphasise that some of the drawings are only the expression of general uncertainty or general neuroticism (figure imbalance, unclear medium line of human figure, legs and arms pressed close to the body, shaded drawing, thickened line or discontinuity of the figure line, and so on), while others are, as a rule, an expression of depression or organic brain disorder (absence of an arm or a leg, i.e. a hand or a foot, body disproportion, above-average small figure or figure very close to the edge of the paper). Some other features of the drawing reveal only the personality outlines, aggressiveness (fingers on extremities), paranoid feature (extremely large drawing with emphasised eyes and ears), or schizophrenia (bizarre drawing with many unusual details, confusion of the *en face* and profile). However, whatever feature of the drawing is concerned, it loses its diagnostic credibility when taken out of the context of other features. This is especially the case when we keep in mind that the features of the human figure drawing may also be influenced by the drawing skill of the subject, which was verbalised by subjects in the test situation very often.

The second step of the choice of the human figure drawing features involved the selection of eight diagnostic categories, to which a number of specific graphical characteristics of the human figure drawing are related. It should be emphasised that the features repeating in two or more diagnostic entities' drawings are not included (although in the first version of methodological preparation, we also selected those features). As for clinical features in a wider sense, the following diagnoses recognisable on the human figure drawing are involved: neurosis, depression, schizophrenia, paranoia, organic disorders, motor deficiency, aggressiveness, and alcoholism. We took the following features from Berger (1984), also paraphrased in that sense by L. Kron (1993), which are related to the diagnoses related to the human figure drawing: neurosis, depression, schizophrenia, paranoia, and organic disorders. On the basis of our own evaluation and insight into the works of other authors, we added three additional diagnostic categories: motor deficiency, alcoholism, and »aggressiveness« as a personality feature.

Table No. 24 presents specific features of the drawing related to all of the eight selected diagnostic categories.

Table No. 24: Diagnostic Features in the Human Figure Drawing

DIAGNOSTIC CATEGORY	GRAPHICAL FEATURES OF THE DRAWING
Neurosis, (general, anxious, hysterical and obsessive)	- figure drawn in the corner or very close to paper edge - small figure - drawing with many details - eye resembling to button - weak figure line - discontinued line of the drawing
Depression	- fragile figure - figure with too few details - head without mouth - sitting or lying figure - figure at the bottom edge of the paper
Schizophrenia	- thin figure - confusion of en face and profile - disproportional figure details - visibility of internal organs - body limit discontinued
Paranoid feature	- enlarged figure - ear over-emphasised only - eye over-emphasised only - written comment follows the drawing
Psycho-organic disorders	- trembling line of the drawing - face without features - trunk simplified or absent - Human figure as drawn by pre-school children - drawing is sloppy, spotty or untidy
Motor deficiency	- strikingly drawn arms - absence of an arm - strikingly drawn legs - absence of a leg
Alcoholism	- square-built body - unclear lines of the drawing
Aggressiveness	- repetition of details - tightly closed fists - teeth on the drawing - fingers on the extremities

We did not separately evaluate the manners in which subjects drew certain parts of the body (head, parts of the face, neck, extremities, trunk, and so on), which was performed by K. Machover (1965), considering that after the first brief insight into the manner of graphical expression of our subjects, we noted a tendency of stereotyped manner of reaction in the test. In other words, we had the impression that the subject experienced the test in a – to a certain extent – regressive way, as a kind of unplanned,

135

short task to be done, considering it, within the range of other instruments, as an interesting, but less important part of the examination.

Let us conclude that in relation to the original Machover Test, we neglected strictly psychoanalytical interpretations of the drawing (regression, castration, and the like), as well as some other formal aspects of the drawing (topic of action, sequence or perspective of the drawing), insignificant to our research. We selected all of the features of this instrument related to the exploration of general mental health, first of all, related to the potential diagnostic pattern of the mental state of subjects.

b) Research Sample

The sample consisted of 201 subjects. The experimental group consisted of 140 subjects, out of which 109 were refugees from a refugee camp in Krnjača near Belgrade (The camp, briefly speaking, is a provisory one, consisting of huts in which whole families live in a single cramped room, sharing a sanitation system with a dozen other families). Another part of the experimental group, 31 of them, represented somatically traumatised subjects, the patients of the Orthopaedic Department of the University Hospital in Belgrade treated at the end of the '90s.

The control group consisted of 61 subjects from Belgrade, for the same period of time which in its socio-demographic features corresponded to the experimental group subjects.

c) Statistical Data Processing

We applied the procedure of calculating the statistical significance of differences among three groups of subjects (refugees and somatically traumatised subjects, and non-traumatised control-group subjects) in the presence of each of the 24 variables examined. More precisely, we calculated statistically significant differences in the presence of one out of twelve general psycho(patho)logical features of the human figure drawing, as well as features of eight diagnostic categories in three mentioned basic groups of subjects. In consideration of the nature of the sample, χ^2-test was applied for that purpose.

Table No. 25 Socio-demographic features of the sample investigated by Machover Test

SOCIO-DEMOGRAPHIC FEATURE		GROUP OF SUBJECTS							
		Experimental group				Control group		Total	
		Refugees		Somatically traumatized persons					
		f	%	f	%	f	%	f	%
Sex	Male	56	51.4	20	64.5	30	49.0	106	53.0
	Female	53	48.6	11	35.5	31	51.0	95	47.0
Age	20 years and younger	11	10.1	9	29.0	4	6.5	24	11.9
	21-30 years	23	21.1	8	25.8	27	44.3	58	28.9
	31-50 years	34	31.2	5	16.2	10	16.4	49	24.4
	50 years and over	41	37.6	9	29.0	20	32.8	70	34.8
Marital status	Married	73	67.0	17	54.8	29	47.5	119	59.2
	Not married	36	33.0	14	45.2	32	52.5	82	40.8
Family status	Living alone	12	11.0	13	41.9	20	32.8	45	22.4
	Living with partner/family member	97	89.0	18	58.1	41	67.2	156	77.6
Education	Elementary	21	19.3	14	45.2	8	13.1	43	21.4
	Secondary	70	64.2	9	29.0	27	44.3	106	52.7
	College and university degree	18	16.5	8	25.8	26	42.6	52	25.9

137

Research Results

a) General features of the human figure drawing implying potential mental disintegration of subjects

Table No. 26 presents only the general features of the drawing of human figure which in terms of statistical significance differentiated refugees, somatically traumatised and non-traumatised subjects.

Table No. 26: General psychopathological features of the human figure drawing most present in terms of statistical significance in the group of somatically traumatised subjects

GENERAL PSYCHOPATHOLOGICAL FEATURE OF THE HUMAN FIGURE DRAWING	FREQUENCIES AND PERCENTAGE OF PRESENCE OF DRAWING FEATURES IN TESTED GROUPS						FREE-DOM DEGREE	VALUES OF χ^2	DEGREE OF STATISTICAL SIGNIFICANCE
	Refugees		Somatically traumatised persons		non-traumatised persons				
	f	%	f	%	f	%			
Thickened line of the drawing	19	17.4	13	**41.9**	21	34.4	2	10.39	0.05
Unclear medium line of the drawing	13	11.9	6	**19.4**	0	0	2	10.69	0.05
Absence of an arm or a leg	20	18.3	7	**22.6**	0	0	2	13.96	0.01

b) Diagnostic features of the human figure drawing

Out of overall eight specific diagnostic features (neurosis, depression, schizophrenia, paranoid feature, organic disorder, motor deficiency, alcoholism and aggressiveness), the presence of which we were to determine on the basis of the human figure drawing, only two of them differentiated statistically significant responses of three groups of subjects – the features of the drawing concerning »motor deficiency« and »aggressiveness«. The results of this examination are presented in Table No. 27.

DIAGNOSTIC FEATURE OF THE HUMAN FIGURE DRAWING	FREQUENCIES AND PERCENTAGE OF THE PRESENCE OF FEATURES OF THE DRAWINGS IN TESTED GROUPS						FREE-DOM DEGREE	VALUES OF χ^2	DEGREE OF STATISTI-CAL SIGNIFI-CANCE
	Refugees		Somatically traumatised subjects		Non-traumatised subjects				
	f	%	f	%	f	%			
Motor deficiency	7	6.4	5	**16.1**	1	1.6	2	7.13	0.05
Aggressiveness	26	**23.9**	6	19.4	1	1.6	2	14.29	0.01

c) Samples of the human figure drawing illustrating significant psychopathological features or diagnostic categories of subjects

For the purpose of better comprehension of the results in the above quantitative re-search performed by a Machover Test application, we shall present drawings of cer-tain subjects – our intention being to illustrate, by means of the image itself, the es-sence of the statistical research results.

First of all, we shall present the key results of this research by presenting appro-priate drawings. Key results are related to human figure drawing features related to general psychopathological features. As pointed out in the above text, these three drawing features are significantly most present in the group of somatically traumatised subjects.

139

Drawing No. 1: Drawing of »human figure with thickened lines«, indicating (as well as shading or absence of line) jeopardised body scheme, which is by this feature either denied or emphasised – the drawing of a 43-year-old person with injured leg

Drawing No. 2: »Unclear medium line« on the drawing of a wounded subject with spinal injury, declared I category invalid

Drawing No. 3: »Absence of an arm or a leg«, drawing of a disabled soldier from the Republic of Srpska with diagnosis of ›Paraplegia‹

Drawing No. 4: »Motor deficiency« on the drawing of a 38-year-old subject injured in a traffic accident, disabled, diagnosed with ›Paraplegia‹ and subsequently treated

Drawing No. 5: »Aggressiveness« as a personality feature on the drawing of a refugee from the Republic of Srpska Krajina, the property of whom was completely destroyed in the war conflict

The following human figure drawings are selected as illustrations of eight examined diagnostic entities, taken from our research material not on the basis of their significantly emphasised quantitative presence (although, no doubt, all of them were registered), but due to their qualitative illustration of the research methods and results on the whole.

The drawings related to diagnostic categories significantly more present in previous quantitative research procedures (»motor deficiency«, »aggressiveness«) were not presented this time, as they were already presented earlier in the study.

Drawing No. 6: Figure of a male neurotic subject, 48-year-old refugee

Drawing No. 7: Figure of a depressive female subject, 48-year-old refugee

Drawing No. 8: Self-image of a schizophrenic subject, 58-year-old refugee

Drawing No. 9: Drawing of a younger paranoid subject from a control group

Drawing no. 10: Figure of a 60-year-old subject with psycho-organic disorders

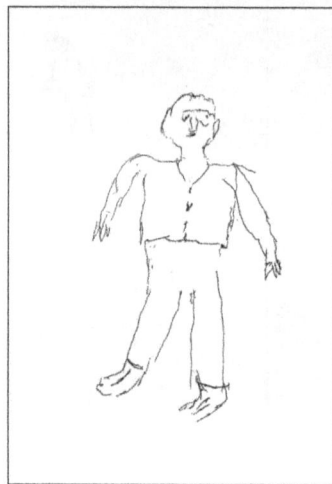

Drawing no. 11: Figure of a 65-year-old subject treated for acute chronic alcoholism

Discussion

As presented in Table No. 26, only three out of 16 general features are, in terms of statistical significance, more present in one out of three tested groups. The »unclear medium line on the drawing« is more significantly present in the group of somatically traumatised subjects. This feature belongs to a domain of general, i.e. relatively undefined, neurotic features of the human figure drawing. In an existential sense, an »unclear medium line on the drawing« in the group of traumatised persons, especially those somatically injured, might be interpreted as weakening of spatial support, which is, on the other hand, existentially bound to the loss of internal orientation in relation to the experience of the whole body. In other words, it can be interpreted as a subjective graphical hint of endangered mental integrity of subjects in general.

Another feature – »absence of an arm or a leg« – is also significantly most present in the group of somatically traumatised persons. It is mainly a sign of motor deficiency and less often of a depressive mood. If the latter is the case, it seems that most frequently, a hand or a foot are missing. »Absence of an arm or a leg« is a clear expression of a disordered body scheme. Therefore, it is understandable that it is most present in the group of somatically traumatised persons. This result, by all indications, represents a grapho-motoric expression of the subjective experience of physical loss of a body part, and when refugees are concerned, it possibly indicates a visual expression of the threat to one's existence, that is, mental integrity of subjects in general. In a narrower sense, the »absence of an arm or a leg« may represent an existential expression of »being riveted« to a certain area, a sort of immovability in space (leg loss), that is, an expression of existential frustration, i.e. inhibition in achieving the project of existing (in subjects using an injured arm at work – in cases of manual professions, or in cases of intellectuals using their hand for writing).

The third feature significantly more present in drawings – the »thickened line« – is, in terms of statistical significance, also most frequently present in the group of somatically traumatised persons. This result implies that this human figure drawing feature is an integrating element of body scheme of the subject, and, as expected, significantly registered as such in subjects whose body integrity is directly jeopardised (somatically injured). A significant role in it may be played by the mechanism of overcompensation (to use Adler's expression), i.e. additional mental investments (psychoanalytically speaking) into the limits of directly jeopardised corporality as unavoidable existential categories in protecting mental integrity of subjects.

As a conclusion, we may say that three out of eight general psychopathological features – »thickened line of the drawing«, »unclear medium line of the drawing« and »absence of an arm or a leg« – are statistically significantly more frequently present in the group of somatically traumatised subjects, while two of them (»unclear line of the drawing« and »absence of an arm or a leg«) are most frequently present in the group of refugees. This result supports the thesis that graphic examination convincingly registers a general existential threat very closely connected with the destruction of physical existence integrity, while the property loss and forced change of social environment, both typically related to refugeeism, play a less important role.

It is interesting that the feature »thickened medium line of the drawing« is the second frequently most present in the group of non-traumatised subjects, after that of somatically traumatised ones. This result raises the question, whether »thickened line of the drawing« expresses the firmness of ego limits or poses the expression of neurotic need to emphasise these limits. However, it seems that after all, the above-mentioned feature of the drawing is, in somatically traumatised subjects, a response of the existence to physical disintegration, that is, the expression of the need for graphically emphasised body limits when jeopardised.

As presented in Table No. 27, »motor deficiency« is, as a feature, most frequently present in the group of somatically traumatised subjects. This result confirms our third hypothesis that somatic trauma, i.e. injuring or wounding at war or in peacetime, has effects on the experience of corporality, i.e. the body scheme, which may be registered graphically. Uzelac (1973) obtained similar results when testing patients suffering from vascular brain insult (hemi-paresis) in comparison to neurotic and normal subjects, and the finding was that 20% of the patients suffering from brain insult fully »incorporated« their motor deficiency into their own body scheme, while 40% of them did so only partially. We agree with his basically psychoanalytic interpretation that traumatic shock caused by somatic trauma in a way refocused libido energy towards the diseased organ of the body, which in time may cause a different, also psychopathological, preoccupation with the diseased organ.

It is interesting that none of other psychiatric diagnoses or personality features (neurosis, depression, schizophrenia, alcoholism, paranoid feature, or mental changes due to organic ones) were significantly more present in the group of traumatised subjects – refugees or somatically traumatised subjects.

Only »aggressiveness«, either as a constant personality feature or as a learned social behaviour, or as a possible sign of acting out, that is, the expression of motor abreaction of internal conflict, is significantly most present in the group of refugees. It is difficult to say if it can be explained by the feature of the (military) mentality of Serbs expulsed from the former Republic of Srpska Krajina, or, according to Cvijić (1931) by Dinaric psychological type, characterised by emphasised impulsiveness. As a matter of fact, a critical percentage of the same mentality, i.e. behaviour, is, in our opinion also present in other two groups of subjects, including, of course, the control group of non-traumatised persons from Belgrade, among whom there is today the highest percent of settlers. Let us add that in the testing situation, when refugees seem to be more dejected, slightly distant and resigned, although ready for cooperation, this may be explained by suppressed mental energy of both libidinous and aggressive nature. Helpless in expressing their aggression towards the main cause of their misfortune – the enemy who is not there (in their minds the enemy is still the main cause of their misfortune), while at the same time their friends may have forgotten or neglected them, refugees very rarely or never have the opportunity to express their aggression towards external objects, especially not towards those who help and support them with their solidarity and otherwise. It is important to note that those people usually pose the only or the most frequent social contact refugees have.

Whatever the case may be, taking everything into consideration it seems that what dominates is suppressed aggressiveness (visible from outside as passiveness, reservedness and hardly noticeable exasperation), which may be revealed only by projective techniques. It is not out of question, however, that similar results would not be obtained by means of some other, non-projective psychometric instruments, which was the case with Serbian researchers (Čavić 2000; Nikolić-Balkoski, Leposavić, Duišin, Milovanović 2002) who obtained similar result, and some foreign authors who tested mental consequences of long-term stress (Hume, Summerfield 1994).

Somatically traumatised subjects, who take the second place in relation to (suppressed) aggressiveness, are, due to their physical handicap, most probably in a situation where they depend on others. Therefore, they have to rely on an additional control of aggressive impulses (which they used to express at motor plan), now initiated by forced motor inactivity.

By application of this method, we did not determine a more significant presence of either less serious mental disorders (neurosis, depression) or more serious ones (schizophrenia, alcoholism or paranoia) in all three groups of our subjects.

Conclusion

The application of the Machover Test led us to the following conclusion: out of the total number of 16 general psychopathological features of human figure drawing, only the following three were significantly more frequently present in our subjects: »thickened line of the drawing«, »unclear medium line of the drawing«, »absence of an arm or a leg« – in all three cases, in somatically injured subjects in comparison to refugees and non-traumatised subjects. Such a finding indicates the ability of the human figure drawing to register the signs of the body scheme disorder in a graphical and projective sense.

The application of the Machover Test also showed a statistically significant differentiation of only two out of eight diagnostic features of human figure, such as »motor deficiency« in somatically injured subjects and »aggressiveness« in refugees. While the former result indicates yet another one out of all of the determined signs of body experience disorder, the graphically registered »aggressiveness« in refugees implies the projective diagnostic abilities of this instrument.

In short, it was confirmed that the Machover Test may identify, through the graphical projection of subjects' total mental status, some general signs of mental change, that is, existential problems of subjects traumatised in various ways.

Resume

The Human Figure Test of the Machover Test is used in the research of projective aspects of the mental status of subjects, especially those with an assumed body scheme disorder. The instrument was adjusted to our research with eight diagnostic categories (neurosis, depression, schizophrenia, paranoid feature, psycho-organic damage, motor deficiency, alcoholism and aggressiveness) with appropriate graphical features in the drawing, and sixteen features of the drawing implying a general disturbance of the mental integrity of subjects mainly of neurotic character (line discontinuity, thickened line, shaded drawing, drawing asymmetry and so on).

The test involved 201 subjects, out of which 109 were refugees from a refugee camp in Krnjača, 31 were somatically traumatised patients from the Orthopaedic

Department of the University Clinic, Belgrade, and 61 were subjects from Belgrade who denied any traumatic experience whatsoever.

By means of an appropriate statistical procedure (χ^2 test) in determining the significance of the presence of 24 features of the drawing in the three tested sub-groups, the following was determined:

- *Out of the general psychopathological features, »thickened line of the drawing«, »unclear medium line of the drawing« and »absence of an arm or a leg« were, in statistical sense, significantly most present in the group of somatically traumatised subjects, thus supporting the hypothesis that the Machover Test examined projective aspects of a disorder of the body scheme experience.*

- *Out of the eight diagnostic categories, only »motor deficiency« was significantly differentiated – of course, in the group of somatically traumatised subjects –, while »aggressiveness« was differentiated in the group of refugees (as an aspect of personality feature), in which, we assume, it was being suppressed.*

The results obtained were commented on within an existential-analytical theoretical framework and compared with the results obtained in similar research.

V

Life Histories of Subjects

1. Life Histories of Refugees

P.M., 48, electrical engineer, Serb, left Šibenik, Croatia and took refuge in Serbia, currently living with her two sons, 15 and 17, in Smederevo on a meagre and irregular salary and the financial support of her sisters, who live abroad.

She grew up in the country, in a harmonious family. »I gladly remember my childhood«. She was a good pupil and a good student, but never disregarded playing and, in her youth, entertainment, dates, sport activities, travelling.

Following her graduation, she worked in Zagreb, Croatia for 4 years, then in Šibenik, Croatia, and, shortly in Novi Sad, Serbia. She is currently employed with a construction firm »Jugovo«, in Smederevo, Serbia, but since the firm is in a very unfavourable condition, has not received her salary and is to be made redundant.

She left Šibenik with her children during her annual holiday, believing she would be returning shortly when the situation had settled, but never returned. What followed was a series of moving from place to place: to Switzerland, to Knin, the former Republic of Srpska Krajina, then to Smederevo, Serbia. Currently she lives in her sister's house. Her husband, who, according to her own words, »earned diabetes« in the meantime, came to Serbia later on. The children's marks at school worsened significantly over the years, »probably due to our moving around and changing environment«.

Beside organic disorders, obviously of psychosomatic character (hypertension, hormonal disorders and spondylitis of the upper part of her vertebrae), she developed manifestations of depressiveness accompanied by bad mood, insomnia and mental tension, which were the reasons she sought professional help. The above-mentioned problems appeared after she became a refugee, preceded by a realistic fear of the massacre in Šibenik by the beginning of the 90's. »The media kept on blazoning that Serbs should be slaughtered, expelled and the like. Šibenik is a town of ethnically mixed population, meaning that there were a lot of Serbs living in it. Our neighbours, who had been our friends until the whole thing started, ignored us, assaulted and offended us. What followed were notices of dismissal from work, reduction of our salaries, then barricades, and finally, the whole madness of war«, says P.M.

In her bad mood and apathy, she dreams about the time of her expulsion very often, and often wakes up in fear and cramps. She very often dreams about the Knin bombing; this became intensive especially during NATO bombing of Yugoslavia in 1999.

Z.B., 30, forestry technician, Serb, left Knin in August 1995. Lived for some time in a refugee camp, now »manages« on her own, by renting a flat. Relations with her family have been disturbed for a long time, mainly with her parents, and partially with her sister.

She often had quarrels with her parents during her childhood. Her father »liked drinking«, had conflicts with everyone, was rude and aggressive. Things were similar concerning her education, which she took to be stressful, precisely speaking, accompanied by constant fears. Following her secondary education, she changed jobs several times, mainly unrelated to her qualifications; most of them were part-time jobs, so that nowadays she officially has almost no years of service.

»During ›Oluja‹ (»Storm«, campaign of Croatian forces to seize Republic of Srpska Krajina and expel Serb population) I ran out of the house during a night, wearing nothing but my pyjamas. Grenades were falling like rain-drops. Then followed days spent in kilometres-long columns of people running away from their homes. When I remember it all, I wish I could not think of anything«, she describes the expulsion.

»No wonder I had to ask for professional help, including neuro-psychiatrists, although what helped me most was bioenergetics... I often suffer from the feeling of groundless fear, tension, which disappear only from time to time«.

Especially following the expulsion, she had unpleasant dreams in which Croats were chasing her, although she admitted having had dreams with the contents of persecution even prior to the expulsion.

»I don't feel bad now. What affects me most is the financial crisis, the feeling of hopelessness«, this young refugee ends her life story.

Z.V., 26, salesman, Serb, single, lives with his father and mother. Since he is unemployed, he is supported by his parents, that is, lives on their pension and what was left of their family savings.

Following a peaceful and happy childhood in Bihać in a regular family environment, he completed his elementary education but had to interrupt his secondary education due to the war that broke out. »It was difficult, we went through all sorts of calamities – hunger, poverty, persecution, expulsion.... I dare not even remember the details... I literally escaped Croatian and Moslem knife by a hair's breadth«. He saved his mother and grandmother by breaking front line with a tractor and driving all the way to the free territory in Bosanski Petrovac.

»We would have hardly survived as refugees if it were not for the humanitarian aid which still remains the basic source of our living«, he describes his current material situation. He lives with his parents in a flat without running water.

In the meantime, according to his own words, he developed a »reactive psychosis«, more precisely, a state of confusion characterised by fear and the intensive experience of being persecuted, which, on the longer run, did not leave more significant traces on his mental state. »Truthfully speaking, I often dream of the scenes of murder, blood, running away from persecution, but I also have ›positive‹ dreams, for example, that I live in peaceful times, without violence, in prosperity, healthily and happily«, this young man concludes his short life history.

D.P., 42, higher medical technician, Serb, left Knin during 1998, single, lives alone. His two sisters with their families remained in the Republic of Croatia. He is currently employed with a trade firm, performing a job unrelated to his qualifications.

He had a difficult childhood, as his parents constantly had conflicts due to his father's behaviour and alcoholism – in the drunken state his father was often violent, throwing his family out of the house, threatening, even beating his mother.

After several years of public mistreatment by his Croat neighbours and colleagues, D.P. was dismissed from work due to his Serb ethnicity, followed by the arrest by the Croatian army despite his being a civilian. He was then sent to a Croatian prison, physically tortured and mentally molested, and »like a delirium«, it lasted around six months.

He does not remember having any serious illnesses until two years ago, when bad mood gradually appeared, leaving him withdrawn, suffering from insomnia, waking up at night often and thinking about the pointlessness of living. He dreams »difficult« dreams with the experience of being persecuted, dreams related to the expulsion he suffered. He often wakes up in cold sweat, with palpitations and the feeling of fear.

Being currently employed, he is satisfied with his social status. If it were not for his milder mental problems of anxiety and his depressive nature, due to which he decided to seek professional help, which proved to be very helpful later on, he would consider his life a normal one.

P.S., 48, Serbian language and literature teacher, had to leave Daruvar in 1991, where he had lived with his two daughters and wife in a village but worked in the town.

He had to take refuge in Serbia before the war conflicts due to the »political persecution of Serbs which he himself felt«. He worked for a period of time as a teacher in a refugee camp in Budva.

He spent his childhood almost idyllically, in the country, living with his parents, who were teachers. He was an excellent, and later very good pupil, had many hobbies (music, pigeon breeding, etc.). Following his secondary education, he worked as a Serbian language and literature teacher in elementary schools in Slavonia.

Immediately following the expulsion, he lived with his relatives for a while but managed to rent an apartment for his family, and, a few year agos, started building his own house.

He has so far been healthy in mental and somatic terms.

He believes that, like the majority of people around him, he is just a bit overly sensitive, and, like everyone else, hopes for better times.

T.Z., 30, forestry engineer, currently living in a rented apartment in Belgrade. She spent her childhood in Slovenia, in an environment in which she always felt lonely. She grew up in a family in which her mother was »like her friend«, while there was »a constant gap« in her relations with her father, especially when he was drunk, as he from time to time suffered from a drinking problem. An alcoholic, he mistreated and abused her mother.

»When thinking about my childhood, I remember playing by the sand box, aware of the poverty of emotional relations with my environment, although I was very open to other Slovenian children«. She read a lot, and was a good pupil and student. As of her relations with the opposite sex, she found them even more difficult, as she was also very shy. »I also had the complex of being too skinny«.

She arrived in Belgrade to study and lived in a student dormitory while her parents had to take refuge in Serbia in 1995. »I personally was not expulsed from Slovenia, but I know what it is like not to know where your parents and your brother are. I was so worried, as I didn't know if they were alive at all, that I could not study as I was supposed to. After their expulsion, I began to feel like a refugee myself«.

She has occasionally been visiting her psychiatrist, due to her bad mood and unspecified fear. »My doctor helped me with some talk and some medicines«.

Nowadays she dreams very rarely, and when it happens, for example, after a heavy dinner or due to high temperature, she has pleasant dreams, of erotic scenes with young men or possibly leaving her parents' home to start a life on her own.

S.R., 58, merchant, divorced, refugee from Sanski Most, of mixed Serb-Moslem origin, currently living in Stara Pazova, without employment, lives on the financial support provided by her brother from abroad.

She had to leave her homeland with her two daughters in 1995. The elder daughter married later on and lives with her husband elsewhere, while the younger also lives elsewhere, with her father.

She describes her childhood as a peaceful and happy one, although her father died when she was eight. Following her successful secondary education, she found employment and immediately got married.

She unwillingly remembers her expulsion. »It was horrible, may it never happen again«. She does not even remember anything related to refugee trauma.

Until three years ago, she was practically mentally and somatically healthy, when she, for the third time, experienced separation from her beloved ones (first from her father, then from her homeland, and finally, from her daughters when they left home). Insomnia, bad mood, gloomy thoughts, sometimes followed by suicidal ones, were the symptoms of her disturbed mental state. She also withdrew from other people, could not eat and mainly spent her time in bed. Only after a longer period of time did she seek professional help. Professional help did bring about some improvement, although she is still not »her old self«.

»I used to live a normal, happy life. Nowadays, as a refugee, I live in misery and suffering«, says this depressive refugee in the conclusion of her bleak life history.

2. Life Histories of Somatically Traumatised Subjects

Š.F., aged 50, highly qualified electrician, Serb form Belgrade, employed for some time at ›Elektroprivreda‹. A divorcee with two children, he lives in the same household as his mother.

He has been treated at the Clinic of Orthopaedic Surgery for the consequences of the closed fracture of the left femur. He was injured three weeks before his emergency admission when a large trunk of black locust fell on his leg.

He ›waited for the surgery‹ for ten days, that is, he underwent a diagnostic evaluation to be subsequently operated under general anaesthesia, and an internal fixation was performed. No complications ensued.

The injury was inflicted at about 7 p.m., after a whole day of heavy work. He had not eaten during the whole day because he wanted to finish the job in one day, as he had promised his girlfriend.

Before the injury, he was never seriously sick. He sustained some of the childhood diseases. He remembers that at the age of 5, he had high fever with sinking sensation. A year before the fracture, he had also had fever, i.e. a sore throat. In the spring time, he usually suffered from colds, accompanied by malaise and sub-febrile body temperatures.

He notes with content that he has no financial problems. He owns three houses and a flat. He rents a house and flat and does not complain of any of the economic problems currently common to the majority of people. He was a moderately successfully student, not too ambitious; however, he was always communicative. He served in the army without any problems. He was initially employed as an electrician in the army, and 25 years ago, due to disputes and machinations at the workplace, he found another post at ›Elektroprivreda‹.

His first marriage broke apart after eight years because he was too ›soft‹ as a husband. ›She left me because, as she said, she was suffocating in the marriage. She was free to go anywhere she wanted and to do anything she wanted, which was not good for the marriage‹. His second marriage failed because his wife was unwilling to leave Budva, where she had lived with her son before marriage, while the third was divorced because he ›was more committed to her children that to his own‹, as he said. ›And love cannot live very long in such situations‹, he briefly comments on his last marriage. He has an adult son from his first marriage who lives abroad and his relations with him are relatively good.

Currently, he has parallel relationships with two women. He claims to be in love with the first one; however, she is married. With the other one, with whom he lives and has an illegitimate girl, he claims to have good relations. He broke his leg working at her summer house.

He is generally satisfied with his hospital treatment. His friends and family visit him. ›I have almost got used to immobility and I am looking forward to going home‹.

V.G., aged 24, butcher of Hungarian nationality from a village near Kovin, where he lives with his father. He has been treated at the Clinic of Orthopaedic Surgery for imjuries of the right femur and shin injuries due to complications in the blood vessels of the same extremity resulting from a traffic accident injury.

V. was delivered by Caesarean section. His mother left them (him as a baby, his older brother and sister and father) and went to work in Germany. His father never remarried, and they were raised by their grandmother on their father's side. As a child, he frequently suffered from sore throats and pneumonia and therefore, at the age of four, underwent in-patient treatment at Pancevo hospital. In spite of his high achievements at school, he decided to go to vocational school and be trained as a butcher. He has been constantly employed with the same boss, being satisfied with his job and wages.

He completed his army service in Kosovska Mitrovica without any problems. He had a girlfriend; however, he broke up the relation after the accident in spite of the fact that they had spent three years together.

As he was prone to drinking, he was nicknamed ›Bottle‹. He usually got drunk on pay day. Sometimes he would spend more money for drinks than he had earned for the whole month, frequently paying the rounds for the whole bar. In spite of this, he never thought of himself as an alcoholic.

He broke his leg in 1998 in a traffic accident. He was drunk, on his way home after a night at a bar, driving his friend on a motorcycle. At the road crossing he bumped into another car, whose driver was also drunk (they both sued one another). Immediately after the accident he underwent a surgical procedure and extension. Due to the vascular complications he underwent another procedure at the II Surgical Clinic. Amputation was also considered; however, his vascular system recovered in the meantime. His last admission to the Clinic of Orthopaedic Surgery was the result of the postoperative wound infection. The infection is resolved and his condition is now good. He walks with crutches and goes out downtown. He is pleased with his treatment and hopes to recover soon.

R.F., aged 46, former hotel manager, graduated from the College of Tourism and Catering, Serb from Sarajevo (Ilidža), father of two adult daughters, lives in Belgrade with his wife and older daughter.

Treated for the diagnosis of quadriparesis with the injury of the third cerebral vertebra. His lower limbs are actually completely paralysed while his right hand is partially paralysed. At the same time, he is incapable of controlling his sphincter and his libido is present only in traces.

He was injured on July 1st, in Neđarići near Sarajevo, during the battle when his helmet suddenly slipped down to his eyes. At that moment, he hit his head against the tunnel beam while running into it to find shelter. As he says, he fell down instantly, however, remained conscious. For the moment, he lost the sensation of his whole body except his head. ›Suddenly, there was nothing, no legs no arms‹, he describes his condition at the time. The paramedics arrived soon and immobilised him, and he was transferred to Belgrade's Military Medical Academy (MMA). His treatment was based only on infusions; no surgical or other orthopaedic procedures were applied. The complications were rather common for the type of injuries developed later on, including the ossification of the right hip joints, and urethral tract calculi. Due to the latter, he underwent lithotripsy on three occasions and eventually lost his right kidney. He was hospitalised in several institutions – the Orthopaedic at Banjica, the Rehabilitation Centre in Melenci, and he spent the longest period in Sokobanjska, where we found him. He believes that rehabilitation has shown results only during the last year and a half. He is capable of walking if assisted, as he says, ›Just like Tinman from the Wizard of Oz‹, adding ›If only my arms were healthy I would walk unassisted using the crutches‹.

R. as a younger child in his family, grew up in a village in Herzegovina. ›My mother gave birth to me at home, and on the same day she went to the field to guide a horse. When she came back I was soaked in blood. My umbilical cord was untied, I was told, and God knows how I survived‹.

During his childhood he suffered from ill health. He was operated on for the inguinal hernia. ›As I remember I frequently received injections due to different diseases, and before school, I was already hospitalised several times‹. However, since his 7th year of age he has been healthy. He was excellent in school and rather successful at college. Additionally, he was a fine athlete and politically active.

He married out of love. His older daughter recently had meningoencephalitis and developed a consequential hearing impairment. ›This was the moment in my life when I went crazy. Neither war, nor wounds, immobility, hospitals and similar things shook me as deep as my daughter's disease‹, says R. In the course of the war in the former Yugoslavia he spent 3.5 years as a volunteer in the army of the Republic of Srpska Krajina. He mostly participated in evacuation and not directly in clashes. In Bosnia, he was one of the organisers of the Serbian uprising in Ilidža. He was a member of the Serbian guard as a commanding officer of an action squad. ›Out of 72 solders in our squad, even 38 were killed, while 70% of the survived were wounded. We went where nobody went ... and still, I regret those days. We were motivated to fight for Yugoslavia, and only later for the Serbian cause. Unfortunately, Ilidža was given to Moslems. I left a house there, two business premises and several hectares of my land. None of us want to go back there. The hardcore Moslems from Sandzak and Srebrenica have settled on Ilidza, and listen to me, the whole family of my mother was slaughtered there during the WWII. Ustashas slaughtered my uncle and my grandparents on my mother's side. In 1992, my mother told my brother and myself: ›Do not let them slaughter you, fight and take care of your next of kin‹, he says.

R.F. continues with his reminiscences on his near past, concluding: ›As for my stay here, I am still full of life, I love everything. Occasionally I spend most of my time reading, or watching movies. I have enough money. Company is not bad. I only feel bad when the weather is poor. Well, things are what they are. And you should know, I would do the same again.‹

P.Z., 32-year-old technician from Laktaši near Banja Luka, Serb, single. Until recently, lived with his parents (who subsequently died, mother in 1998, at the age of 54, father in 1997, at the age of 57). Presently he lives alone.

He had been treated for the diagnosis of paraplegia consequential to the injury of the 11th and 12th thoracic vertebra. He was injured in Western Slavonia, somewhere between Pakrac and Lipik. ›It was during the action intended for the evacuation of our people. Someone had made a mistake. We came almost to the centre of the village, and were forced to retreat. I was hit with a dumdum bullet in the abdomen, most probably fired by a sniper, since it was a single shot. My guts, lungs, spine, liver and who knows what else were torn apart. I was told that it was a miracle that I lived‹. He was transferred from the battle filed to Bosanska Gradiška, where he underwent first aid management. Thereafter, he was transported by helicopter to the Military Medical Academy in Belgrade, where he underwent more than 12 surgical procedures. ›My lungs were operated three times, spine two times, bed sores three times. I was also in Igalo, at home, on several occasions‹. My rehabilitation program is currently in progress. I exercise regularly and I am very pleased with my physical therapists. As a child of guest workers, P. was born in Ebigen in the Federal Republic of Germany. He said that he had always been naughty. His mother always had two jobs, while his father worked as a stoker in a factory, and since they had built the house in Bosnia in the meantime, they decided to come back to Yugoslavia.

He told us that he had, before the war, had affairs with several girls. ›At the time when I was injured, I had already spent six months with one of them. After the accident, I stopped calling her. I let her go. Later on, I heard that she got married and had a baby. Believe me, now I have only one aim - to find a girl and start a family. I have tried to be with girls. However, they keep leaving me - I cannot achieve an erection. I have tried with certain injections. I can do anything that a healthy man can, but stubbornness kills us. What should I say, I have suffered greatly, P says, hardly capable of hiding his disappointment in his current existential situation.

Finally he adds that at the beginning of the war, his mother tried to talk him into going to Germany and avoiding mobilisation since he had German citizenship. ›However, I had a feeling of obligation to my father's land. Whatever it is, you have a duty

159

to fulfil. I cannot be compared to those who were in the war for 4-5 years. I only spent three months on the battlefield. To tell the truth, I was the victim. I do not condemn those who ran away. It looks now as if they have been smarter. After all, I think that I would do the same again, but I will try to be more careful, I would not be so reckless. That is youth.‹

F.B., aged 26, technician of mixed nationality from a small town in Vojvodina. Divorced and lives alone. Father of two children, five-year-old son and 3-year-old daughter, who live with their mother in Germany.

He has been treated for a year with the diagnosis of *paraparesis spastica* resulting from the injury of the first lumbar and twelfth thoracic vertebra.

Immediately after his birth, his mother (of Ruthenian nationality on her father's side and Hungarian on her mother's side) threw him into a ditch in order to ›hide her sin‹ since she had conceived the child with a foreigner – an Austrian, who had left her only after several months of living together. He was saved by his grandfather who raised him as an Orthodox with a great deal of tolerance toward other confessions (it is to be mentioned that he also has three half sisters on his father's side whom he has never met, and another two sisters and a brother on his mother's side from her second marriage). At the age of three, he took over his mother's maiden name since his father had never asked for him. He barely made passing grades in the elementary school, while his grades in the high school reached the level of ›very good‹. ›I never met my father, my mother rarely visited me, my grandmother was unable to express her love. My grandfather was the only one who loved me, and of course I loved him very much, although, later on, he got to love my sisters more than me. At the age of 15, I decided to become independent and to recognise God as my only superior. Unfortunately, at the time I came into contact with bad company. I had joined a sect of Satanists in Zrenjanin, participated in their ritual sacrifice of animals and reached the level of the master of the third degree. I left them, believing only in three sacrednesses - God, children and nature. The latter remained from them. You know, when I left the sect I was followed by a red dog for a long time ...‹, R. completes his adolescent story on searching for his identity.

Since the age of 11 he has had sexual relations with older women. He met his wife in a coffee shop, and after a while they were married because she was pregnant. The marriage lasted two years. He believes that the divorce was caused by his wife's depression and diabetes which developed after her father's death. He sends alimony regularly, although his wife's financial situation is rather good and she does not depend on his money since she has been working in Germany.

When the war broke out in 1992 he happened to be in Herzegovina in regular army service in the sabotage units. At the time, he was wounded for the first time when artillery shell inflicted contusions all over his body on him. ›For seven months I

160

went where nobody else dared to go. I have fourteen souls on my conscience. It destroyed me completely. When I completed my service, my life became chaos. I had an irresistible desire for destruction. I kept breaking the furniture, stabbing a knife into the doors, I broke all of the windows, etc. I was impossible. At the time, I spent several days at the Department of Psychiatry at the Military Medical Academy. I did not know who I was or where I was. I nearly strangled my own brother and killed a good friend‹, R. tells the story of his first war experience.

Thereafter, he settled down and started to attend churches in order to ease his conscience. ›I was in several of them, even in some sects.‹ He finally settled at the Pentecostal church. ›An alcoholic talked me in. He told me that God loves everybody, regardless of their sins. I liked that, although at the beginning I had hard times accepting all their stories. Finally, I settled down. I found a job and my wages were good.‹

›When the bombarding of Yugoslavia started, I enlisted as a volunteer to defend my country, in the front lines.‹

He was wounded by a blast bomb fragment on Košare in Kosovo. On the occasion, he saved his friend by pushing him down, which enabled him to avoid deadly shell fragments. The remaining eight soldiers were killed. He says: ›When I tried to get up after the explosion, I realised that I was not able to. I touched by trousers, and realised that my legs were there; however, I was unable to move them. I saw blood and stopped the haemorrhage as I had been trained before. Bushes around me were burning. I decided to move and take with me my wounded and unconscious friend. I also took my rifle with me with the idea of killing myself if things became too hard. However, later on, I abandoned that idea again because I believed that suicide was a deadly sin. At night, my wounded friend still unconscious, I talked to myself – creepy. In the meantime, he regained his consciousness. He was able to move, and went for help. They came to take me at dawn. They carried me to Junik in a tent half, and later on in a car to Priština, where I was immediately operated.‹ Thereafter, R. was transferred to Niš hospital, and two days later to the Military Medical Academy in Belgrade. Among others, a bomb fragment was pulled out of his spine. He was on the rehabilitation program in Melenci and in Sokobanjska street. In the meantime, due to the indwelling catheter (mandatory in paraplegics), he developed renal calculi and thus underwent lithotripsy.

By the end of the two-hour conversation, a nurse came by and reminded him to mention that he was awarded the order of a national hero and a medal in the field of national defence and security. R. confirmed that reluctantly, leaving an impression of a restless and distracted man and, above all, a person who has not talked as much as he should.

T.K. 50-year-old housewife from Belgrade, Serb, completed elementary school, lives with her brother's family.

She has been treated at the Clinic of Orthopaedic Surgery for the fracture of the right ankle. At the time of this interview she was in a plaster cast.

As a little girl, she was a lively child. She was told that as a baby, she had had chicken pox. At the age of four, she fell off a stool and lost her consciousness. Ever since, she has been treated for epilepsy. In the past, her fits (of the grand mal type) were more frequent (once a week). However, currently they have been considerably rare, and they are associated with sudden weather changes or southern wind. She has no sexual experience, nor relations with boys. ›I had wanted to be free ever since I knew what the boys were like‹, says T.

She lived in the same household with her parents until 1992, when she fled from Sarajevo to Belgrade. She now lives with her brother's family, where she works as a housekeeper since her brother and sister-in-law are both employed. Her mother died of the consequences of starvation immediately after they came to Belgrade in 1995. She reads a lot, mostly biographies and travel reports.

She was injured on her way to the library. She slipped on the ice on the pavement and fell on her back.

Finally, she adds that occasionally she hears voices, mostly neutral or encouraging, telling her, ›You must endure, be patient, you will win.‹ Earlier, before the application of the antiepileptic drug Mazepine, on several occasions she experienced visual hallucinations (skeletons, different monstrous faces). Currently, she is free of these psychotic symptoms, which tended to occur alternatively with her fits. (She was diagnosed as having Landolt's epilepsy, with hallucinant psychotic episodes lasting for several minutes occurring alternatively with major epileptic fits).

After the admission to the Clinic of Orthopaedic Surgery she was afraid of not being able to walk again, however the doctors reassured her: ›I feel safe here and I believe doctors. I must succeed. I read biographies, which are also encouraging. I am only concerned with respect to drugs since I have increasing difficulties in providing them‹, this ›ethereal individual‹ – as she was called by her former therapist Dr. Radmilo Jovanović (a famous psychiatrist and also a refugee from Bosnia) in his impressive Ph.D. thesis – completed her story.

Z.K. Aged 70, night watchman, Serb, refugee from Grahovo in Bosnia. Currently he lives with his wife in a village near Kikinda in a rented house.

He has been treated at the Institute of Orthopaedic Surgery, CCS for a right femur fracture.

The fifth of eight children, he was raised in a family of farmers. As a child he was healthy. Later on, he was operated on for appendicitis, and subsequently for inguinal hernia as well. He has five children (three sons and two daughters), all of whom are married and independent. Two of them are having a hard time as refugees in Belgrade while the other three are not doing too well either. He fled before the ›Storm‹, saving the head on his shoulders. He says, ›Everything I had was burnt to the ground, four cows, 50 sheep, 30 lambs, tractor, reaper, two trailers. Ustashas burnt down more than 90% of the village.‹ He has visited Grahovo five times so far. In his house, which is largely preserved, a Croatian police officer from Imotski lives now. He has decided to go back because he believes that neither he nor his family have any future here.

He was injured while he was riding a bicycle in his village. He was tired, on his way back from work. The tractor driver who knocked him down and threw him into a ditch was careless and did not have a driver's license. Immediately after admission, he underwent a surgical procedure and an external fixture was applied. Six months later, he underwent another procedure for correction and for the pain which has been present ever since the accident. He still has pains, although he uses analgesics unwillingly.

When he was asked to describe his dreams, he refused to do that: ›What should I describe when I have nothing‹. Since I understood him, I did not insist.

Literature

Aćimović B. (1998): Stavovi Beogradjana prema izbeglicama, diplomski rad, Filozofski fakultet, Beograd.

Adamović V. (1984): Telesne bolesti i emocije, Nolit, Beograd.

Ahrens S., Hasenbring M. (1991): Warum Psychosomatik in der Orthopädie? in: Willert H.-G., Wetzel-Willert G. (Hrsg): Psychosomatik in der Orthopädie, Huber V., Bern-Stuttgart-Toronto, 36-41.

Alečković-Nikolić M. (1998): Etno-psihološki pratragovi psihoterapije: slovensko-pagansko i istočno hrišćansko nasledje, Psihoterapija, 2, 76-82.

Asmundson G., Norton R., Allerdings M., Norton P., Larsen D. (1998): Posttraumatic Stress Disorder and Work-Related Injury, Journal of Anxiety Disorder, 12 (1), 57-69.

Atanasijević G. (1996): Uticaj sociodemografskih faktora i kumulativnog efekta stresnih životnih dogadjaja na izbor mehanizma prevladavanja stresa kod žena sa izbegličkim statusom, diplomski rad, Filozofski fakultet, Beograd.

Bärbel Z. (1998): Stressreaktion und soziale Kompetenz, Inauguraldissertation zur Erlangen des Doktorgrades, Fakultät Psychologie und Pedagogie, München.

Barrett D. (Ed) (1996): Trauma and Dreams, Harvard University Press, Harvard.

v. Bayer-Katte W. (1995): Soziale Marginalisierung und systematische Desintegration als Methode des Meinungsterrors, in: Behnke K., Duchs J. (Hrsg): Zersetzung der Seele, Rotbuch V., Hamburg, 84-101.

Becker D. (1997): Trauerprozess und Traumaverarbeitung im interkulturellen Zusammenhang, in: Wirtgen W. (Hrsg): Trauma-Wahrnehmen des Unsagbaren, Roland Asanger V., Heidelberg, 23-39.

Behnke K., Fuchs H. (Hrsg) (1995): Zersetzung der Seele, Psychologie und Psychiatrie im Dienste der Stasi, Rotbuch V., Hamburg.

Berger D. (1997): Zdravstvena psihologija, Društvo psihologa Srbije - Centar za primenjenu psihologiju, Beograd.

Berger J. (1984): Psihodijagnostika, Nolit, Beograd.

Bernal E. W. (1984): Immobility and the Self: A clinical-existential Inquiry, Journal of Medicine and Philosophy, 9(1), 75-91.

Biesold K.-H. (2000): Wenn nichts mehr ist wie früher..., Extracta psychiatrica, 3, 24-28.

Bischoff C., Zenz H. (Hrsg) (1989): Patientenkonzepte von Körper und Krankheit, Huber V., Bern-Stuttgart-Toronto.

Boss M. (1985): Novo tumačenje snova, Naprijed, Zagreb.

Buydens-Branchey L., Noumair D., Branchey M. (1990): Duration and Intensity of Combat Exposure and Posttraumatic Stress Disorder in Vietnam Veterans, The Journal of Nervous and Mental Disease, 178(9), 582-587.

Cartwright R. D. (1991): The Relation of Dream Incorporation to Adaption to Stressful Events, Dreaming, 1 (1), 3-9.

Cashman L. A., Dijkers M. P. (1990): Depressed Mood in Spinal Cord Injured Patients: Staff Perceptions and Patient Realities, Arch. Phys. Med. Rehabilitation, 71, 191-196.

Crveni Krst Srbije (1998): Izbegli i prognani - gde i kako žive, Humanost, 7, 11-12.

Cvijić J. (1931): Balkansko poluostrvo i južnoslovenski narodi, knjiga 2, Beograd.

Čajkanović V. (1973): Mit i religija u Srba, Beograd.

Čavić T. (2000): Izbeglice u kolektivnom smeštaju, u: Vlajković J. Srna J., Kondić K., Popović M. (ur.): Psihologija izbeglištva, IP »Žarko Albulj«, Beograd, 129-138.

Čavić T. (2002): Psihološki problemi izbeglica, u: Marić J. (ur.): Mentalno zdravlje izbeglog, raseljenog i prognanog stanovništva, Institut za psihijatriju KCS, Beograd, 37-43.

Davis G. C., Breslau N. (1994): Post-traumatic Stress Disorder in Victims of Civilian Trauma and Criminal Violence, Psychiatric Clinics of North America, 17(2), 289-299.

Delimar D., Sivik T., Delimar N., Korenjak P. (1998): Posttraumatic Stress Disorder among Croat Soldiers in the D. War in Croatia 1991-1993., Stress Medicine, 14(1), 43-47.

Denis D., Eslam J., Priebe S. (1997): Psychische Störungen nach politischer Inhaftierung in der sowjetische Besatzungszone und der ehemaligen DDR von 1945-1972, Fortschritte der Neurologie und Psychiatrie, 65(11), 524-530.

Deserno H. (1995): Träumen, Übertragen und Erinnern, in Bareuther H. et al. (Ed): Traum und Gedächtnis, 3. Internationale Traumtagung, 16.-18. März, 123-151.

Desimirović V. (1997): Trauma i traumatsko iskustvo, u: Vlajković J., Srna J., Kondić K., Popović M.: Psihologija izbeglištva, Nauka, Beograd, 59-69.

v. Dijk C. N., Besselaar P. B., Marti B. K., Strubbe W. (1991): Konversion oder orthopädisches Problem? in: Willert H.-G., Wetzel-Willert G. (Hrsg): Psychosomatik in Orthopädie, Huber V., Bern-Stuttgart-Toronto, 206-209.

Dimitrijević I., Rašković-Ivić S., Velimirović S., Banovac J., Milovanović V., Oklobdžija S. (2002): Procena mentalnog zdravlja izbeglog, prognanog i raseljenog stanovništva, u: Marić J. (ur.): Mentalno zdravlje izbeglog, raseljenog i prognanog stanovništva, Institut za psihijatriju KCS, Beograd

Drozdek B. (1997): Follow-up Study of Concentration Camp Survivors from Bosnia--Herzegovina: The Years Later, The Journal of Nervous and Mental Disease, 185, 690-694.

Dyregrov K., Dyregrov A., Raundalen M. (2000): Refugee Families Experience of Research Participation, Journal of Traumatic Stress, 13(3), 413-426.

Dzioba R. B., Doxey N. C. (1984): A prospective Investigation into the orthopaedic and psychologic Predictors of Outcome of first lumbar Surgery following Industrial Injury, Spine, 9(6), 614-623.

Erić Lj. (2000): Psihoanaliza i psihopatologija likovnog izraza, Institut za mentalno zdravlje, Beograd.

Esposito K., Benitez A., Barza L., Mellman T. (1999): Evaluation of Dream Content in Combat-Related PTSD, Journal of Traumatic Stress, 12(4), 681-687.

Farlane A. (2000): Etnoculturale Issues, in: Nutt D., Davidson J., Zohar J. (ed): Post-Traumatic Stress Disorder: Diagnosis, Management and Treatment, Dunitz, London, 187-198.

Feiereis H. (1983): Die psychosomatische Dimension bei Erkrankungen der Bewegungsorgane, in: Studt H. H. (Hrsg): Psychosomatik in Forschung und Praxis, München-Wien-Baltimore, Urban und Schwarzenberg, 411-430.

Feinstein A., Dolan R. (1991): Predictors of Post-traumatic Stress Disorder following Physical Trauma: An Examination of the Stressor Criterion, Psychological Medicine, 21, 85-91.

Filipović V.(1996): Uslovi života u Centru za kolektivni smeštaj izbeglica, diplomski rad, Filozofski fakultet, Beograd.

Flatten G., Hofmann A., Liebermann P., Wöller W., Siol T., Petzold E. (2001): Posttraumatische Belastungsstörung, Schattauer, Stuttgart-New York.

Fontana A., Rosenheck R., Horvath T. (1997): Social Support and Psychopathology in the War Zone, The Journal of Nervous and Mental Disease, 185, 675-681.

Freud S. (1948): Die Traumdeutung, Ges. Werke II/III, Imago, London, 1-643.

Globus G. G. (1991): Dream Content: Random or meaningful?, Dreaming, 1 (1), 27-40.

Hamner M. B. (1994): Exacerbation of Posttraumatic Stress Disorder Symptoms with medical Illnes, General Hospital Psychiatry, 16 (2), 135-137.

Hartman E. (1991): Dreams that Work or Dreams that Poison? What does Dreaming do?, Dreaming, 1 (1), 23-25.

Hećimović V., Supek-Ilić D., Kulović S. (1992): The Wounded Soldier, in: Klain E. (Ed): Psychology and Psychiatry of a War, Faculty of Medicine, Zagreb, 118-137.

Hendin M., Haas A.P. (1984): Combat adaptations of Vietnam veterans without posttraumatic stress disorder, American Journal of Psychiatry, 141, 956-960.

Hobson J. A. (1998): Dreaming as Delirium: A Replay to Bert States, Dreaming, 8 (4), 10-15.

Hopf H. H. (1992): Geschlechtunterschiede in Träumen - Inhaltanalytische Erfassung von oknophilen und philobatischen Traumbildern in den Träumen von Kindern und Jugendlichen, Praxis Kinderpsychologie und Kinderpsychiatrie, 44 (5), 176-184.

Hume F., Summerfield D. (1994): After the War in Nicaragua: A Psychosocial Study of War Wounded Ex-Combatants, Medicine and War, 10, 4-25.

Ilić V. (2001): Between Integration and sustainable Return Refugees in Serbia, Helsinki Committee for Human Rights in Serbia, Belgrade.

Jäckel W., Cziske R., Andres Ch., Schochat Th., Jacobi E. (1989): Subjektive und objektive Kriterien mit Erkrankungen der Bewegungsapparats, in: Bischoff C., Zenz H. (Hrsg): Patientenkonzepte von Körper und Krankheit, Huber V., Bern--Stuttgart-Toronto, 115-123.

Jakulić S., Krstić M. (1994): Silovanje kao psihotrauma u ratnim uslovima, u: Kaličanin P., Bukelić J., Išpanović-Radojković V., Lečić-Toševski D. (ur): Stresovi rata, IMZ, Beograd, 161.

Jatzko H., Jatzko S., Seidlitz H. (1995): Das durchstossene Herz-Ramstein 1988, Verlagsgesellschaft Stumpf-Kossendey, Edenwecht.

Jin H. Q., Araki S., Wu X. K., Zhang Y. W., Yokohama K. (1991): Psychological Performance of Accident-Prone Automobile Drivers in China: A Case-Control Study, International Journal of Epidemiology, 20(1), 230-233.

Jovanović A. (1997): Ratne psihotraume i porodica, Zadužbina Andrejević, Beograd.

Jovanović A., Pejović M., Marinković J., Dunjić D., Aleksandrić B., Nadj I. (1996): Uticaj socioekonomskih faktora na nivo opšteg životnog funkcionisanja obolelih od posttraumatskog stresnog poremećaja, Engrami, 18, 47-54.

Jovanović A., Pejović M., Vranić K., Radotić M. (1997): Psihosocijalna studija amputiraca žrtava rata 1991-1995 u bivšoj SFR Jugoslaviji, Association to Aid Refugees, Margo Art, Beograd.

Jovanović R., Djurović S. (2002): Problemi socijalizacije ranjenika i psihosocijalni aspekti ranjavanja u: Preradović M., Raičević R., Špirić Ž. (ur): 70 godina Vojne psihijatrijske službe, Javno preduzeće PTT Srbije, Beograd, 98-102.

Jovanović Z. (1994): Izbeglice i njihov smeštaj u Republici Srbiji 1991-1993, u. Kaličanin P., Bukelić J., Išanović-Radojković V., Lečić-Toševski D. (ur): Stresovi rata IMZ, Beograd, 31-38.

Kaličanin P., Bjelogrlić M., Petković I. (1992): Teški psihički poremećaji izazvani stresovima rata, studija 356 hospitalizovanih pacijenata u 9 psihijatrijskih ustanova, Institut za mentalno zdravlje, Beograd.

Kaličanin P., Lečić-Toševski D., Bukelić J., Išpanović-Radojković V. (1994): Predgovor, u: Zdravlje pod sankcijama, Institut za mentalno zdravlje, Beograd, 11-16.

Kimball Ch. P. (1985): To Sleep, Perhance to Dream, in: Achté K., Tamminen T. (ed): The Psychopathology of Dream of Sleeping, Psychiatria fennica - Suplementum, 112-116.

Klain E., Vidović V. (1992): The »Suspicious« Citizen, in: Klain E.: Psychology and Psychiatry of a War, Faculty of Medicine, Zagreb, 185-190.

Klajn H. (1995): Ratna neuroza Jugoslovena, Tersit, Beograd.

Kron L. (1993): Kajinov greh - psihološka tipologija ubica, Prometej - Institut za kriminološka i sociološka istraživanja, Beograd.

Kuhn W., Bell R., Seligson D., Laufer S., Lindner J. (1988): The Tip of the Iceberg: Psychiatric Consultations in an Orthopaedic Service, International Journal of the Psychiatry in Medicine, 18(4), 375-382.

Künsebeck H.-W., Lempa W., Freyberger H. (1984): Identification of psychosomatic and psychic Disorders in non-psychiatric In-patients, Psychotherapy and Psychosomatic, 42(1-4), 187-194.

v. Laer L. (1991): Der Einfluss der ärtzlichen Psyche auf das Soma des Patienten, in: Willert H.-G., Wetzel-Willert G. (Hrsg): Psychosomatik in der Orthopädie, Huber V., Bern-Stuttgart-Toronto, 215-220.

Lansky M. R., Karker J. E. (1989): Post-traumatic Nightmares and the Family, Journal of Clinical Psychiatry, 11 (2), 169-183.

Lazarus R.S. (1996): Psychological Stress and the Coping Process, New York.

Leposavić Lj., Nikolić-Balkoski G., Milovanović S., Barišić-Rojnić J., Barac Z. (2002): Mentalni problemi porodice u izbeglištvu, u: Marić J. (ur.): Mentalno zdravlje izbeglog, raseljenog i prognanog stanovništva, Institut za psihijatriju KCS, Beograd, 89-96.

Levin R., Galin J., Zuwiak B. (1991): Neightmares, Boundaries and Creativity, Dreaming, 1 (1), 63-74.

Machover K. (1965): Personal Projektion in the Drawing of the human Figure, Charles C. T-Publisher, Springfield, Ilinois.

Macklin M., Metzger L., Litz B., McNally R., Lasko N., Orr S., Pitman R. (1998): Lower Precombat Intelligence is a Risk Factor for Posttraumatic Stress Disorder, Journal of Consulting and Clinical Psychology, 66(2), 323-326.

Marinković N. (1993): Stories from Hell (Confessions of Serbs tortured in the Concentration Camps in Croatia and Bosnia and Herzegowina in 1991 und 1992), Beograd.

Marković A. (1973): Ekspresivni pokreti, grafomotorna produkcija i crtež ljudske figure, Kliničke sveske, 1-2, 11-18.

Marković Z., Jovanović A., Vranić K. (1994): Psihosocijalne konzekvence poremećaja telesne sheme kod pacijenata sa amputacijom ekstremiteta, Engrami, 16(1-2), 41-44.

Milivojević Lj. (1998): Transfer i kontratransfer u grupnoj psihoterapiji, doktorska teza, Medicinski fakultet, Beograd.

Milosavljević M. (1997): Socijalni aspekti izbeglištva, u: Vlajković J., Srna J., Kondić K., Popović M.: Psihologija izbeglištva, Nauka, Beograd, 9-20.

169

Mitić M. (1997): Porodica, zdravlje i bolest, u: Berger D.: Zdravstvena psihologija, Društvo psihologa Srbije - Centar za primenjenu psihologiju, Beograd, 217-243.

Mitrović D., Popov I., Vlajković K., Krstić V. (1994): Mentalno higijenski aspekti zbrinjavanja izbeglih lica, u: Kaličanin P., Bukelić J., Išpanović-Radojković V., Lečić-Toševski D. (ur): Stresovi rata, IMZ, Beograd, 89-102.

Morina B.: Priče iz kolona u Srbiji, Public Press, Kraljevo 1997.

Nikolić-Balkoski G., Leposavić Lj., Duišin D., Milovanović S., Lasković N. (2002): Problemi mentalnog zdravlja i bolesti starih u izbeglištvu, u: Marić J. (ur.): Mentalno zdravlje izbeglog, raseljenog i prognanog stanovništva, Institut za psihijatriju KCS, Beograd, 97-103.

Noble D., Roudebush M.-E., Price D. (1952): Studies of Korean War Casualties; Part I - Psychiatric Manifestations in Wounded Men, American Journal of Psychiatry, 108, 495-499.

Nyberg E., Frommberger V., Berger M. (1998): Die Posttraumatische Belastungsstörung: Grundlagen, Klinik und Therapie, Extracta psychiatrica, 12(10), 21-24.

Opalić P. (1988): Egzistencijalistička psihoterapija, Nolit, Beograd.

Opalić P. (1990): Das Verhältnis zwischen den gesellschaftlichen Faktoren und der Entstehung der Neurosen, Medizin, Mensch, Geselschaft, 2, 115-124.

Opalić P. (1992): Istraživanja posledica ratnih trauma u prethodnoj Jugoslaviji, Engrami, 21 (2), 41-45.

Opalić P. (1998): Da li je moguća analiza prethodne Jugoslavije kao male grupe, Gledišta, 1-2, 150-159.

Opalić P. (1999): Analiza snova u grupi, u: Ilanković N. (ur): Svest, spavanje, snovi, Institut za psihijatriju KCS, Beograd, 189-198.

Opalić P. (1999): Untersuchung zur Gruppenpsychotherapie, Psychosozial Verlag, Giessen.

Opalić P. (2000) Research of the Dreams of the Traumatised Subjects, Psihijatrija danas, 32 (2-3), 129-147.

Opalić P. (2000). Stres i telesna trauma, Sociologija, 2, 193-204.

Opalić P. (2000): Dreams in Traumatic Reality, Reflections, Long Beach, 6 (2), 30-35.

Opalić P. (2000): Istraživanje snova traumatizovanih, Psihijatrija danas, 2-3, 149-165.

Opalić P. (2000): Psihoterapijska pomoć izbeglicama u Jugoslaviji do 1998., Sociologija, 4, 637-697.

Opalić P. (2003): Socijalno-psihijatrijski aspekti izbeglištva iz Hrvatske i Bosne i Hercegovine u SRJ, u: Krestić V. (ur): Zbornik o Srbima u Hrvatskoj 5, SANU, Beograd, 287-305.

Opalić P., Djamonja T., Nikolić G., Barišić-Rojnić J. (1997): Grupna psihoterapija shizofrenija sa empirijskom evaluacijom, Avalske sveske, Institut za psihijatriju KCS-a, Beograd.

Opalić P., Lešić A. (2001): Ispitivanje psihopatološkog stanja pacijenata sa povredama muskuloskeletnog sistema, Medicinska istraživanja, 35, 1, 10-16.

Opalić P., Lešić A. (2001): Psiha i telesna trauma, CIBIF, Medicinski fakultet, Beograd.

Opalić P., Panović V. (1991): Istraživanja značaja faktora stresa za pojavu neuroza, Sociologija, 4, 523-536.

Orr E., Aronson E. (1990): Relationships between orthopaedic Disability and percevied social Support: Four theoretical Hypotheses, Rehabilitation Psychology, 35(1), 29-42.

Papić Ž. (1992): Telo kao »proces u toku«, Sociologija, 23(2), 259-274.

Peltzer K. (1995): Ethnokulturelle Konzepte von Trauma und deren Behandlung, in: Peltzer K., Aycha A., Bittenbinder E. (Hrsg): Gewalt und Trauma, IKO-Verlag für interkulturelle Kommunikation, Frankfurt, 208-225.

Peltzer K. (1995): Trauma im Kontext von Opfern organisierter Gewalt, in: Peltzer K., Aycha A., Bittenbinder E. (Hrsg): Gewalt und Trauma, IKO-Verlag für interkulturelle Kommunikation, Frankfurt, 12-36.

Peretz L., Kaminer H. (1991): Dreams that Poison Sleep: Dreaming in Holocaust Survivors, Dreaming, 1 (1), 11-21.

Petković I. (1994): Terapijske intervencije u prevenciji i ublažavanju psihosocijalnih posledica stresa, Institut za mentalno zdravlje, Beograd.

Petronijević B. (1998): Psihologija, Zavod za udžbenike i nastavna sredstva, Beograd.

Petrović B., Popović V., Dabović C., Proročić S., Dobrijević I. (1994): Zlostavljanje uhapšenih i zarobljenih lica - specijalni oblik ratnih stresova u gradjanskom ratu u Jugoslaviji, u: Kaličanin P., Bukelić J., Išpanović-Radojković V., Lečić-Toševski D. (ur): Stresovi rata, Institut za mentalno zdravlje, Beograd, 149-159.

Pflüger P. M. (Hrsg) (1992): Gewalt warum, Walter V., Olten.

Plog U. (1995): Vertrauen ist gut - Über den Mißbrauch der Psychiatrie durch den Staatssicherheitsdienst in der DDR, in: Behnke K., Fuchs J. (Hrsg): Zersetzung der Seele, Rotbuch V., Hamburg, 284-295.

Polovina N., Divac Lj. (1992): Posttraumatski stresni poremećaj i psihoterapijski pristup, Vojnosanitetski pregled, 49 (2), 115-125.

Popov I., Mitrović D., Stokić S. (1994): Porodica u izbeglištvu, u: Kaličanin P., Lečić-Toševski D., Bukelić J., Išpanović-Radojković V. (ur): Zdravlje pod sankcijama, IMZ, Beograd, 89-106.

Popov R., Pećanac M. (1985): Akutno napito stanje kao uzrok saobraćajnog traumatizma na petogodišnjem materijalu, u: Zbornik radova Sekcije za saobraćajnu medicinu SLD, Beograd, 106-107.

Popović M. (1994): Neki aspekti psihološke pomoći izbeglicama u Srbiji, Psihijatrija danas, 26 (2-3), 241-244.

Popović M. (1999): Snovi u analitičkoj psihoterapiji, u: Ilanković N. (ur): Svest, spavanje, snovi, Institut za psihijatriju KCS, Beograd, 177-188.

Potts M. K. (1994): Long-term Effects of Trauma: Posttraumatic Stress among Civilian Internees of the Japanese during World War II, Journal of Clinical Psychology, 50(5), 681-698.

Pražić B. (1971): Crtež kao prilog dijagnostici u psihijatriji, Anali Kliničke bolnice »Dr M. Stojanović«, Zagreb, 10, 9.

Priebe S., Bolze K., Rudolf K. (1994): Andauerende psychische Störungen nach Represalien infolge eines Ausreiseantrages in der damaligen DDR, Fortschritte Neurologie und Psychiatrie, 62, 433-437.

Priebe S., Denis D. (1998): Leiden bis heute - über die psychische Folgen politische Verfolgung in der DDR, Nervenheilkunde, 17, 84-90.

Ranković T. (1997): Sociološka analiza načina života izbeglica u kolektivnom smeštaju u Krnjači, diplomski rad, Filozofski fakultet, Beograd.

Raphael B., Lundin T., Weisaeth L. (1989): A Research Method for the Study of Psychological and Psychiatric Aspects of Disaster, Munksgaard, Copenhagen.

Ringel E. (1991): »Was kränkt, macht krank«, in: Willert H.-G., Wetzel-Willert G. (Hrsg): Psychosomatik in der Orthopädie, Huber V., Bern-Stuttgart-Toronto.

Rudić N., Rakić V., Išpanović-Radojković V., Bojanin S., Lazić D. (1994): Deca i mladi u izbeglištvu u kolektivnom smeštaju, u: Kaličanin P., Bukelić J., Išpanović-Radojković V., Lečić-Toševski D. (ur): Stresovi rata, IMZ, Beograd.

Rudolf G. (2000): Psychotherapeutische Medizin und Psychosomatik, G. Thieme V., Stuttgart-New York.

Schade B., Schunk T., Schüffel W. (1998): Stress and Stress-Reactions of Members of the German Forces in Peacekeeping Missings: Health Promoting and Health Detrimental Factors, Centre of Internal Medicine, Phillips University, Marburg.

Schenck C. H., Mahowald M. W. (1991): Injurious Sleep Behavior Disorders (Parasomnais) Affecting Patients on Intensive Care Units, Intensive Care Medicine, 17 (4), 219-224.

Schilder P. (1950): The Image and Appearance of the human Body, I International University Pres, New York.

Schmitz P. (1978): Medizinische Literatur zum Traumbild, Arbeiten der Forschungsstelle des Instituts für Geschichte der Medizin der Universität zu Köln, Band 10, Köln.

Schreuder B. J. N. (1995): Posttraumatic Re-enactment in Dreams, in: Bareuther H. et al. (Ed): Traum und Gedächtnis, Neue Ergebnisse aus psychologischer, psychoanalytischer und neurophysiologischer Forschung, 3. Internationale Traumtagung, 16-18. III 1995, 187-203.

Schreuder B. J., Kleijn W. C., Rooijmans H. G. (2000): Noctural Re-experiencing more than forty Years after War Trauma, Journal of Trauma Stress, 13 (3), 453-463.
Schüffel W. (1987): Ärtzlicher Einsatz im Katastrophenfall, Grubenunglück Stolzenbach - Borken, Hessische Ärzteblatt, 1, 27-29.
Schumacher M. (1995): Supervision im Kontext von bosnischen Vergewaltigungsopfern, in: Peltzer K., Aycha A., Bittenbinder E. (Hrsg): Gewalt und Trauma, IKO-Verlag für interkulturelle Kommunikation, Frankfurt, 193-207.
Schunk T., Schade B., Schüffel W. (1998): Evidence for the Predominance of Resource-Factors in the Context of Stress in Missions Abroad, Department of Psychosomatic Medicin, Centre of Internal Medicine Phillips-University Clinik, Marburg.
Self Help Line (1999): Sleep Matters, Medical Advisory Service, London.
Ships J. G., Coburn F. E. (1945): Psychiatric Study of One Hundred Battle Veterans, War Medicine, 8, 235-237.
Solomon Z., Mikulincer M. (1987): Combat Stress Reactions, Post-Traumatic Stress Disorder and Somatic Complaints among Israeli Soldiers, Journal of Psychosomatic Research, 31(1), 131-137.
Srna J. (1997): Nasilje, u: Vlajković J., Srna J., Kondić K., Popović M. (ur): Psihologija izbeglištva, Nauka, Beograd, 117-123.
Srna J. (1997): Psihološka pomoć pojedincima i porodicama ugroženim ratom, u: Vlajković J., Srna J., Kondić K., Popović M.: Psihologija izbeglištva, Nauka, Beograd, 149-153.
Stepansky R., Holzinger B., Schmeiser-Rieder A., Saletu B., Kunze M., Zeitlhofer J. (1998): Austrian Dream Behavior: Results of a representative Population Survey, Dreaming, 8 (1), 32-45.
Stojanović J. (1999): Snovi - od simbola i mitova do istorije ljudske civilizacije, u: Ilanković N. (ur): Svest, spavanje, snovi, Institut za psihijatriju KCS, Beograd, 161-176.
Stojanović Lj. (1973): Primena projektivnih crteža u kliničkim uslovima, u: Kliničke sveske, Društvo psihologa Srbije, 1-2, 3-7.
Svetska zdravstvena organizacija: ICD-10 Klasifikacija mentalnih poremećaja i poremećaja ponašanja, Zavod za udžbenike i nastavna sredstva, Beograd, 1992.
Špirić Ž., Samardžić R., Mandić-Gajić G., Bjelica N. (2002): Posttraumatski stresni poremećaj i komorbiditet, u: Preradović M., Raičević R., Špirić Ž. (ur.): 70 godina vojne psihijatrijske službe, Javno preduzeće PTT Srbije, Beograd, 55-62.
Taylor S. (1986): Health Psychology, Random House, New York.
Todorović J. (1973): Evaluacija crteža ljudske figure kao testa ličnosti u odnosu na pristup i iskustvo, magistarski rad, Filozofski fakultet, Beograd.

Trijsburg R. W. (1989): Träume als Anzeichen von Veränderungen der Alexithymie bei psychosomatischen Patienten, Psychotherapie, Psychosomatik, Med. Psychologie, 39 (12), 471-475.

v. Uexküll T. (1996): Psychosomatishe Medizin, Urban u. Schwarzenberg, München-Wien-Baltimore.

Urbina S. (1981): Methodological Issues in the quantitative Analysis of Dream Content, Journal of Personality Assesment, 45 (1), 71-78.

Uzelac U. (1973): Projekcija prihvaćenosti motornog deficita na Mahover tehnici, Kliničke sveske, Društvo psihologa Srbije, 1-2, 23-32.

Valdetarro A.R. (1997): Aktuelno stanje izbeglica u SR Jugoslaviji, u: Fond - Demokratski centar: Pravni položaj izbeglica, Beograd, 10-15.

Van der Veer G. (1995): Beratung und Psychotherapie mit Opfern organisierter Gewalt, in: Peltzer K., Aycha A., Bittenbinder E. (Hrsg): Gewalt und Trauma, IKO-Verlag für interkulturelle Kommunikation, Frankfurt, 82-97.

Vijay P. M., Shamsundar C., Shivaprakash M. W., Sriram T. G. (1988): Psychiatric Morbidity in Orthopaedic Outpatients, Nimhans Journal, 6(1), 23-26.

Vlajković J. (1997): Psihološka pomoć u krizi, u: Vlajković J., Srna J., Kondić K. Popović M.: Psihologija izbeglištva, Nauka, Beograd, 189-193.

Vlajković J. (1997): Psihološki aspekti izbeglištva, u: Vlajković J., Srna J., Kondić K., Popović M.: Psihologija izbeglištva, Nauka, Beograd, 21-28.

Vlajković J. (1997): Savetovanje, u: Vlajković, Srna J., Kondić K., Popović M.: Psihologija izbeglištva, Nauka, Beograd, 195-200.

Vögele C., Steptö A. (1986): Psychological and Subjective Stress Responses in Surgical Patients, Journal of Psychosomatic Research, 30(2), 205-215.

Vujko M., Kuzmanović E., Božović Lj. (1994): Psihički problemi amputiranih - naša iskustva u radu sa ranjenicima, u: Kaličanin P., Lečić-Toševski D., Bukelić J., Išpanović-Radojković V.: Zdravlje pod sankcijama, Institut za mentalno zdravlje, Beograd, 127-132.

Vukas M. (1994): Uticaj stresa izazvanog ratom i sankcijama na gradjane iz bivše Jugoslavije nastanjene u Švedskoj, u: Kaličanin P., Bukelić J., Išpanović-Radojković V., Lečić-Toševski D. (ur): Stresovi rata, IMZ, Beograd, 103-112.

Watson C. G., Brown K., Kucala T., Juba M., Davenport E. C., Anderson D. (1993): Two Studies of Reported Pretraumatic Stressors Effect on Posttraumatic Stress Disorder Severity, Journal of Clinical Psychology, 49(3), 311-318.

Weine S., Vojvoda D., Becker D., McGlashan T., Hodžić E., Laub D., Hyman L., Sawyer M., Lazrove S. (1998): PTSD Symptoms in Bosnian Refugees 1 Year after Resettlement in the United States, American Journal of Psychiatry, 155(4), 562-564.

Whitlock F. A., Stoll J. R., Rekhdahl R. J. (1977): Crisis, Life Events and Accidents, Australian and New Zealand Journal of Psychiatry, 11, 127-131.

Wilcox J., Briones D., Suess L. (1991): Auditory Hallucinations, Posttraumatic Stress Disorder and Ethnicity, Comprehensive Psychiatry, 32(4), 320-323.

Willert H.-G., Wetzel-Willert G. (Hrsg) (1991): Psychosomatik in der Orthopädie, Huber V., Bern-Stuttgart-Toronto.

Winter H. (1996): Posttraumatische Belastungsstörungen nach Verkehrsunfällen, Peter Lang V., Frankfurt/M.

Wood J. M., Bootzin R. R., Rosenhan D., Nolen-Hoeksema S., Jourden F. (1992): Effects of the 1989 San Francisco Earthquake on Frequency and Content of Nightmares, Journal of Abnormal Psychology, 101 (2), 219-224.

World Health Organisation (1992): Psychosocial Consequences of Disaster--Prevention and Management, Geneva.

Wyshak G. (1994): The Relation between Change in Reports of Traumatic Events and Symptoms of Psychiatric Distress, General Hospital Psychiatry, 16(4), 290-297.

Zenz H., Bischoff C., Fritz J., Duvenhorst W., Keller K. (1989): Das Schicksal von Krankheitstheorien und Behandlungserwartungen des Patienten im Gespräch mit dem praktischen Arzt, in: Bischoff C., Zenz H. (Hrsg): Patientenkonzepte von Körper und Krankheit, Huber V., Bern-Stuttgart-Toronto, 148-160.

2004 · 300 Seiten · Broschur
EUR (D) 29,90 · SFr 52,20
ISBN 3-89806-348-8

Ende der 80er Jahre wurde Jugoslawien in den Strudel tiefgreifender und verwirrender Veränderungen gerissen, deren Folgen nicht abzusehen waren. In diesem Prozess sind aus jungen Männern aktive Kriegsteilnehmer geworden. Dies hat nicht nur ihre Welt verändert, sondern auch ihre Deutung dieser Welt – ihre Begriffe von Krieg und Heimat, Freund und Feind, Sicherheit und Freiheit, Trauma, Kaltblütigkeit und Macht. Wie hat sich dieser Prozess vollzogen? Wie sehen diese Männer sich selbst und ihre Welt kurz nach Beendigung der kriegerischen Konflikte? Wie lassen sich ihre Biografien und Vorstellungen auf der Grundlage der jugoslawischen Welt nach 1945 verstehen? Welches sind die Bedingungen dafür, gegen ehemalige Mitbürger und Nachbarn, verwandt oder fremd, gewaltsam vorzugehen. Diesen Fragen ist Natalija Basic nachgegangen: Sie hat biografische Interviews mit jungen Männern im ehemaligen Jugoslawien geführt und deren Aussagen in ihrer Studie zusammen gestellt und ausgewertet.

P🔲V
Psychosozial-Verlag